VIRTUAL SCHOOLING

VIRTUAL SCHOOLING

A Guide to Optimizing Your Child's Education

Elizabeth Kanna and Lisa Gillis,

with Christina Culver

palgrave
macmillan

VIRTUAL SCHOOLING
Copyright © Elizabeth Kanna, Lisa Gillis, Christina Culver, 2009.
All rights reserved.

First published in 2009 by PALGRAVE MACMILLAN® in the U.S.—a division of St. Martin's Press LLC, 175 Fifth Avenue, New York, NY 10010.

Where this book is distributed in the UK, Europe and the rest of the world, this is by Palgrave Macmillan, a division of Macmillan Publishers Limited, registered in England, company number 785998, of Houndmills, Basingstoke, Hampshire RG21 6XS.

Palgrave Macmillan is the global academic imprint of the above companies and has companies and representatives throughout the world.

Palgrave® and Macmillan® are registered trademarks in the United States, the United Kingdom, Europe and other countries.

ISBN: 978–0–230–61432–1

Library of Congress Cataloging-in-Publication Data
Kanna, Elizabeth.
    Virtual schooling / Elizabeth Kanna, Christina Erland Culver, Lisa Gillis.
        p.   cm.
    Includes index.
    ISBN 978–0–230–61432–1
    1. Computer-assisted instruction.   2. Alternative education.
3. Blended learning.   4. Virtual reality in education.   I. Culver,
Christina Erland.   II. Gillis, Lisa.   III. Title.
LB1028.5.K28   2009
371.33'44678—dc22

                                                            2009000257

A catalogue record of the book is available from the British Library.

Design by Letra Libre

First edition: June 2009
10 9 8 7 6 5 4 3 2 1
Printed in the United States of America.

For

Michael, Randall, Madison, and McKenzie Kanna

&

Scott, Brian, John, Stephen, and Rebekah Gillis

CONTENTS

INTRODUCTION

Bill Gates had them both.

In *Outliers,* Malcolm Gladwell's latest book, Gladwell points out how access and parent advocacy were catalysts for Gates's founding Microsoft and igniting the PC revolution, which he would go on to dominate. It is well known that Gates dropped out of Harvard, but few know that Gates's parents withdrew him from public school because he was bored and enrolled him in Lakeside, an elite private school in Seattle.

That same year the Lakeside Mother's Club put together a rummage sale and spent the proceeds on a computer terminal for the school. This would be standard for today, not in 1968.

The Lakeside computer terminal was a new type of computer that shared processing power with a much larger computer in downtown Seattle. Gates would learn programming without being slowed by the laborious punch-card process used by the majority of computer terminals in existence at the time. Gates's access to the computer terminal had allowed him to get thousands of programming-hours under his belt when he and fellow student and future business partner, Paul Allen, saw the cover of the January

1974 *Popular Electronics* magazine featuring the first do-it-yourself computer kit—the Altair 8800. That time spent programming and gaining knowledge about that rare thing in 1968—a computer— positioned him to seize the opportunity with the Altair 8800 and go on to make history. Writes Gladwell, "Gates got to do real-time programming *as an eighth grader in 1968.*"

What if millions of eighth graders across the United States were given access to burgeoning industries, innovative technologies, and subjects they found exciting? What if their parents advocated for and supported that access?

Gates had parents who fought for their son's needs and access to a new field that few knew about at the time.

The need for this powerful combination of access and advocacy is the reason we wrote this book.

In April 2008, we recognized that a definitive guide to virtual schooling had to be created in order to share with parents the power of access that virtual schooling could give a child. We knew we had to first explain the concept and then define the many approaches out there—from blended models and concurrent enrollment to mobile technology.

Our credentials are rooted in our expertise in the homeschooling movement. Collectively, we have held the titles of president of the board of education, director of government affairs, credentialed teacher, credentialed administrator, virtual school developer, and our jobs include a White House appointment. This background, along with our personal experience as virtual schooling early-adaptors with our own children, uniquely empowers us to be prognostic in defining the education model poised to transform education in the twenty-first century.

This book will show you how virtual schooling got started, where it is today, and, more importantly, where we see its true potential.

That potential is in your child—just waiting to be discovered.

CHAPTER 1

THE EDUCATION OF THE FUTURE— HERE TODAY

It is 7:30 on a Monday morning and McKenzie, age 12, wakes up, kisses her Chihuahua, Ringo, says good morning to her parents, and gets ready to jet off to her classes at an academy that specializes in teaching math, science, and engineering. She attends school on Mondays and Wednesdays, taking classes in pre-algebra, history, and English with 15 other students. Her teachers stay in contact with her, as well as with her parents, by e-mail and a program called SnapGrades, which informs them almost daily about McKenzie's progress.

Thursdays are different for McKenzie. She catches up on work for her classes, works on her weekly history essay with guidance from her tutor via e-mail (and from her dad from his classroom 20 miles away and from her mom who works in a home office), and works on her grammar skills in a self-paced course at Universal-Class.com. Next, McKenzie uses an online math program to help her grasp challenging concepts, reads a chapter in her history book, then meets with her French tutor at a local coffee shop. The meeting is conducted entirely in French since McKenzie hopes to become fluent and one day live in France.

On the same Monday morning McKenzie's 15-year-old sister, Madison, takes her terrier for a walk while she listens to a lecture on psychology from a Pulitzer Prize–winning professor and then a lecture on history from a Stanford University professor, both downloaded from iTunes U to her iPod. Once back at her desk, she puts in a DVD and watches a lecture on geometry for a course. Next she uses her computer to "attend" a class from a self-paced online MIT biology course, then meets with her supervising teacher to review her progress in preparation for the high school exit exam. Later in the day, her language arts tutor, an associate professor at Stanford University who works for the gifted and talented program, meets her at the local park where they discuss *Pride and Prejudice*.

On Tuesdays and Thursdays, Madison, who has a passion for Jane Austen, physically attends a course on British literature at Sacramento State University. The professor acknowledges her during the lecture as the youngest in the accelerated college entrance program's history. On her way home, Madison stops at a special event on campus and she signs up for a workshop for aspiring authors, where she'll share the novel she is writing. At home she meets with a tutor to work on one of her college essays. Later in the day, Madison completes a Chinese language lesson online and e-mails her completed essay to her tutor for final editing.

Their 18-year-old sister, Randall, is now a full-time college student. She graduated from high school a semester early with a year of college credits. One of the highlights of Randall's primary schooling was a special online program, and an actual weeklong expedition, with Robert Ballard, the oceanographer who found the *Titanic*. As Randall was encouraged to optimize technology throughout her elementary and high school years, she is proficient at doing the same as a college student. Driving to her college classes in the morning, she uses the iPhone app Evernote to dictate an essay she'll begin writing back at her laptop that evening. She also uses other iPhone apps such as Study Aid to create customized flashcards, Memoreasy to study more efficiently, and Stanza to access over 25,000 free e-books for class research. Her acumen in combining virtual resources with conventional classroom-based classes has translated into landing a spot on her college's President's Highest Honors list. As Randall moves into her second year of college, she explores many possible career paths. She loves acting and is auditioning for a lead in the college play. She is also on the costume committee and sings in a community music program. The many years of access to passionate mentors and teachers in various fields have given her confidence and have helped her to take these pursuits to the next level. She even has taken steps to launch her own clothing line.

These aren't kids in a futuristic movie or an episode from *Lifestyles of the Rich and Famous*. Nor were these girls playing chess at age two, or acing algebra at age six as they raced on a fast-track academic career to MIT. In fact, math isn't their best subject and they struggle with it, like many kids.

McKenzie, Madison, and Randall's education is an example of how to combine classroom-based and online resources in order to customize a learning plan. The Kanna girls call themselves "virtual schoolers." They take some classes at a public school and use the computer or other technology for another portion of their coursework. Their parents, Elizabeth (co-author of this book) and Michael, have assembled programs from the Internet, the community, and the classroom and created a customized education for their daughters under the auspices of a public school. The public school ensures that the girls meet the state requirements for a high school diploma and issues them reports cards.

The flexibility of their education is thanks to a charter school in California. All the classes, online programs, and services the Kannas have accessed are available through publicly funded schools, school programs, and free or nominal-fee resources online. An education previously reserved for the wealthy is now available to all.

Your children can learn from the smartest people in the world and access the best quality curricula and other innovative public resources that together are creating a revolution in the quality of U.S. education.

TWENTY SCIENCE BOOKS IN ALL OF EUROPE

Somewhere around the year 1449, a man named Gutenberg created a new technology that revolutionized how humanity learned and shared knowledge. The printing press increased literacy and supported an exchange of ideas that previously had been denied to all but a select few.

Virtual schooling is similarly positioned to create a twenty-first-century revolution that will change our society. Like the printing press, virtual schooling gives us previously unavailable access, choice, and power when it comes to shaping our children's education. Whether it is access to the contents of a rare book, the best math curriculum in the world, experts in every field of study imaginable, or AP courses taught at an elite institution, you can utilize today's technology to personalize your child's education according to his or her needs.

Just as Gutenberg's printing press expanded the amount of available information in Europe more than 500 years ago, virtual schooling is creating a revolution in education and an exponential leap in humanity's capabilities.

DIGITAL NATIVES IN NINETEENTH-CENTURY SCHOOLS

If we want to change the wallpaper settings on our smart phone, we turn to our smart 12-year-old instead of trudging through the manual. Our children "speak" the digital language. Having grown up in a digital world, they are digital natives, while we parents are digital immigrants. Growing up with all things digital has made them proficient multitaskers: answering text messages in a new text-speak, often hundreds a day while surfing the Internet, doing their homework, listening to music on their iPod, and checking into their favorite chat room at the same time. They also play video games and online role-playing games, in which a large number of players interact with each other in a virtual world. Growing up digital allows them to understand the language of our new digital landscape.

But we send our "digital natives" to schools created over 150 years ago.

The "common school movement" that Horace Mann, Henry Barnard, and other education reformers created in 1852 was designed for the training of future factory workers. School children were treated like automobiles on a factory assembly line. Teachers and curriculum were the production-line workers, planting information into children before dispatching them to the next station. It was a one-size-fits-all approach, with textbooks, blackboards, and limited learning resources available for children who where headed to factories for their entire work life. That is a period of history that no longer exists and a student that no longer exists.

Today's children learn differently.

They have lived only in a digital world. They learn, communicate and play utilizing digital devices and computers. They require—

and deserve—an education tailored to the digital world they'll work in, far removed from the factories of a distant past.

THE SCHOOL OF THE FUTURE—HERE NOW

According to the International Association for K–12 Online Learning (iNACOL) website (www.inacol.com), online learning is growing at a pace of 30 percent annually and 44 states have significant supplemental online programs. Clayton Christensen, in *Disrupting Class,* states that enrollments in state-accredited online courses went from 45,000 in 2000 to roughly one million in 2007. Christensen estimates that by 2019, less than ten years from now, with a looming shortage of teachers and widespread state budget crises, enrollment in online learning will *surpass* that of live instruction.

Virtual schooling started as a disruptive technology, a technological innovation that improves a product or service in ways that the market does not expect. Because disruptive innovations tend to be simpler and more affordable than existing products, they become the norm within a new market or arena of competition. These innovations start to handle more complicated problems, and then they take over and supplant the old way of doing things. Computer-based learning first became popular for AP classes, rural schools with a shortage of courses or qualified teachers, urban schools in low-income areas, and homeschooling families. Next, several visionary entrepreneurs saw the potential of leveraging this emerging technology to solve complicated problems facing the educational system. Entrepreneurs like Keith Oelrich and Ron Packard. Oelrich, CEO of Insight Schools, founded Insight Schools to help solve the U.S. epidemic of teenage dropouts. Ron Packard, CEO of K^{12}, Inc. founded his technology-based curriculum company to level the playing field of access to a competitive education by offering a world-class curriculum and school to any child with access to a computer and a passion for learning.

Packard and Oelrich faced staunch opposition but held firm in their convictions that virtual schooling was the future of education as did many other virtual schooling innovators like Barbara Dreyer, CEO of Connections Academy and Julie Young, president and CEO of Florida Virtual School. Their independent, yet congruent missions required spending thousands of hours to educate legislators, school administrators, and teachers that public virtual education should and could be an option for every child in the country. A mission they are all still pursuing today.

_____

With the click of a mouse, a child with a passion for learning has the ability to break down barriers imposed by income, race, distance, or their school's limited coursework and class offerings. That innovation is propelling virtual education to develop at breakneck speed. So fast that we don't know how virtual schooling will be defined in the future. Never before have so many options existed for parents and children to leverage the expertise of people and learning opportunities from all around the world.

But the human interaction necessary to educate a child—to engage students, teachers, and parents is the foundation of learning. Regardless of the technological advances for learning, nothing can replace you and your commitment to your child's success.

THE NEXUS OF HUMAN ENGAGEMENT AND TECHNOLOGY

Technology alone won't transform education. Taking our current model of one-size-fits-all education and delivering it from an online-learning school platform or other cutting-edge digital delivery method is like taking a Model T, adding new tires, and hoping it will fulfill the needs of car drivers today. This is a short-sighted attempt at leveraging the benefits of technology for education. Any virtual school program or curriculum must respect how each of its students learns best. We believe this new model of education, virtual schooling, represents the nexus of engaged human involvement and the new delivery method for curriculum and programs.

Accordingly, we define virtual schooling by the potential it holds: We see it as a personalized learning approach accomplished by leveraging the best of virtual and classroom-based schools and programs tailored to a child's needs and interests. Virtual schooling holds the potential to be the twenty-first century educational approach that can best address every child as an individual with a dominant learning style, myriad intelligences, a unique learning pace, and unique aspirations.

A child that is nurtured to respect how he or she learns best, the pace at which he or she likes to learn, along with his or her intelligences, unique talents, and passions, will learn to respect that elegant mix for the rest of his or her life. Christopher Paolini, author of the best-selling *Eragon* book series, graduated from high school at the age of 15 after having participated in an accredited correspondence program. That program allowed him to work at his own pace and afforded him the freedom to explore his love for nature and literature. Now, all children can have that same opportunity.

WHY THE TIME IS NOW FOR ALL PARENTS TO EXPLORE VIRTUAL SCHOOLING FOR THEIR CHILDREN

Across the country, we ask our teachers to do the impossible every day—educate twenty-first-century children in a nineteenth-century-inspired model of education.

All too often, the maxim in public school teaching is "Teach to the middle." This means that the level of instruction and assignments may be too easy for the top third of the class and too hard for the bottom third. The result? The brightest go unchallenged, which leads to distraction. The below-average achiever is overwhelmed, often humiliated and angry, and they, too, gradually check out. Could this student lethargy and "checking out" be part of the dire public school statistics today? According to the Milken Institute, by the year 2015, 80 percent of the world's scientists will come from Asia, contributing to the valid concern that our students are not being groomed and trained for critical scientific careers.

The Average Joe graduating from the factory-model K–12 education system is underprepared to compete in our technology-centric workforce. We send our digital natives to school and many graduate underqualified for a career in technology, forcing U.S. businesses to recruit employees from other countries, or, worse, outsource the work entirely.

Alone, each of these statistics and changes in society is alarming. Collectively, they represent an intellectual crisis. "We need an intellectual change," says Susan Hackwood, executive director of the California Council on Science and Technology and a virtual schooling parent. Whose job is it to fix the growing disconnect between our K–12 education system and the skills our children need to succeed? Is it the government's place, our boards' of Education, or our teachers'? Yes to all of the above, but more than anything, the responsibility is ours. Technology is redefining the way we live. Education is no exception. Gone are the days when we can settle for limiting the involvement in our child's education to helping with homework, joining the PTA and attending school functions. Our children need us to be their advocates to ensure they receive the twenty-first-century education the new workplace demands. While some schools are excellent, not all schools are created equal. No one has a stronger desire to see a child succeed than her parents. Gandhi once said: "Be the change you want to see in the world." America needs our children to be the intellectual change we must see in our world.

VIRTUAL MENTORS: A DIFFERENT LENS TO THE WORLD

Youth in America access the Internet and are quickly inundated with the latest "news" about Paris Hilton and Britney Spears, but how many of them have gone online to read about Richard Sandor? How many have heard about Richard Sandor? Richard Sandor, economist and professor, wrote a prescient paper on how to solve a potentially catastrophic environmental challenge we were facing in the 1970s. His paper was the catalyst for finding a way to solve the acid rain problem. With his collaboration, the Clean Air Act passed and contributed to eliminating the challenge to our environment.

Fast-forward to 1992, when Sandor wrote another paper proposing a solution to global warming. Sandor then launched the first trading system for greenhouse emissions to combat CO_2.

Sandor has made helping save the planet his life's work. Paris Hilton has made being a celebrity, taking advantage of photo opportunities, and attending parties her life's work. But which one does your child know about? How do we protect our children from seeing a limited and dumbed-down version of what is going on in the world and help to expose them to what is truly important? We change the lens they are using. If your teen attends UC Berkeley, they might have an opportunity to learn from Steven Chu, Nobel Prize–winning professor and now the U.S. secretary of energy. Today, any teen with an iPod, iPhone, or iPod Touch can listen to Chu's lectures on solving our energy needs. Does your child have a passion for design or art? The New York Public Library has a miniseries at iTunes U that features artists and designers, from glassblowers to letterpress printers. Mentors can be from the past as well. Einstein's discoveries teaching about time and space are no longer restricted to mentions in your child's textbooks. These are all free video and audio podcasts at iTunes U. By utilizing virtual mentors as part of your virtual schooling with your child, mentors are no longer restricted to a geographic location or an in-person relationship.

The person your child grows up to be will be largely based upon the influences you provide in his or her life. In the past, these great mentors could only be accessed through deliberate trips to the library and hours of research. Through today's virtual learning opportunities, these mentors are now available through a click that transcends barriers of time and geographical limitations. We now have the power to provide the lens that shapes our child's future. What lens is she using for that view?

ACCESS = A+ IN MATH AND SCIENCE

What are the chances technology won't continue to transform our lives, our workplace, and the world? Pretty small. Today, America's 15-year-old students trailed their counterparts from many industrialized nations and were farthest behind in math and science.[1] Experts are unanimous that the teaching of math and science in elementary and high schools needs a critical transformation to keep up with the pace of change in our global economy. Most knowledge-based jobs demand mathematics and science knowledge and abilities. If we are 35th in math in the world and your child is doing "okay" in math in school, you can't assume she'll graduate with the necessary skills to compete in the workplace. Even if your child doesn't have strong aptitudes in science or math or is not exploring a higher education in science and engineering (only 4 percent of ninth graders go on to graduate in science and engineering fields, another critical issue facing the United States), knowledge-based jobs (requiring math and science abilities) made up 85 percent of the jobs created in the last decade. Robert Kotick, CEO of Activision Blizzard, Inc., says that the greatest challenge facing his leading video game company is the lack of properly educated and well-trained potential employees. Regardless of your child's current education, supplementing his or her math and science learning is critical. Fortunately, there are a myriad of great programs online. Your child's study of science isn't restricted to a textbook but can expand out into a virtual lab or MIT lecture. If your child is struggling with an area of math, there are sites like www.yourteacher.com, which offers more than 1,000 lessons, or www.tutor.com, where you pay a reasonable fee per minute for tutoring. Math and science are intrinsically linked to your child's future success, period. Carl Sagan said: "It is suicidal to create a society dependent on science and technology in which hardly anybody knows anything about the science and technology."

WHAT YOU'LL GET FROM THIS BOOK

This book creates, for the first time ever, the overarching definition of this innovative form of education and compiles the most common methods being used today. Your approach can be comprehensive, a full "start-to-finish" curriculum with support, or it can supplement your children's current schooling to prepare them for success. It can also be a "blended approach," a customized education of mixed computer and hands-on classroom-based education. We define various terms being utilized in the market and new approaches to virtual schooling that are not yet defined, so that you have the knowledge to research what is offered and are aware of the requirements and possible supplemental benefits to optimize your child's current education.

Every family is different. As you seek to create a personalized education for your child, your lifestyle and routines will dictate some of the choices you make. You'll learn that flexibility is one of the greatest attributes of virtual schooling, in that you can choose courses of study that work best for your budget and family dynamics while meeting your child's individual needs. The tennis star Maria Sharapova was a typical girl whose physical talents took her out of a seat-based classroom and on the road to realizing a dream. Through enrollment in a virtual school program she was able to combine her schooling with her competition schedules. Maria's education never missed a beat as she pursued her dream of becoming a tennis star who ultimately won Wimbledon. With virtual schooling, children can finish their academic learning in a more condensed time period. This efficiency gives them the extra time to explore their passions and help them enjoy the freedom to excel in the arts, athletics, or academics.

Whether you are a full-time working parent or you stay at home, options exist that will allow you to participate in your child's education. These methods of communication can keep you abreast of your child's progress and able to respond quickly as her needs and interests grow and develop.

We'll explore the seven approaches to virtual schooling and explain how to find schools and programs in your area. For example, in California, the charter school system offers personalized learning charter schools, and, therefore, the ability to maximize the benefits of a hybrid approach, as we saw with McKenzie, Madison, and Randall. The state of Texas has developed a computer laptop program in order to reach migrant populations, and all across the nation, charter programming is becoming accredited as an alternative to traditional public education. As a leader in virtual education, Kansas allows for students to take virtual courses while concurrently receiving certificates in vocational training so that students can graduate with both a diploma and job skills. South Carolina has led the nation in innovative education solutions by establishing a statewide charter school district. In its first months of operation, thousands of students found the opportunity to complete their education virtually under the public system through a network of district-sponsored charter schools. The South Carolina State Department of Education was overwhelmed when just 12 short months after rolling out a supplemental virtual program, over 10,000 had students signed up—and that was just from within the state boundaries alone.

Regardless of where you live, if your child attends public school, private school, or is homeschooled, there are many virtual schooling approaches that can help you to personalize and enhance your child's education. We hope this book will inspire and help you in your search as you navigate all the options virtual schooling has to offer. We also hope it gives you the confidence to be like Guttenberg and join a new revolution in education.

VIRTUAL POWER—IT IS *YOU*

Virtual schooling, regardless of which approach you use, can provide your child with the education of a maverick. And you might feel like a maverick as well. It takes more time, effort, and energy to actively participate in your child's education, but nothing really worth having is easy. Virtual schooling transforms the definition of school from a building with teachers and blackboards and a fixed set of courses to infinite possibilities for learning and your child's future. Virtual schooling isn't a panacea for all of the educational challenges facing America. It does, however, give you and your child access to the brightest minds in the world and the latest innovations to optimize your child's learning. Utilize the virtual schooling resource guide in Chapter 8 of this book or online at www.ivirtualschool.com to supplement your child's current education or explore the possibility of a full-time virtual school, personalized learning charter school, or hybrid school that keeps your child engaged, passionate about learning, and always reaching for her full potentials. As a parent, you have given the most important gift to humanity—our future.

WAIT! THIS ALL SOUNDS OVERWHELMING . . .

Two authors of this book are parents. We have jobs, aging parents, spouses, children (even teenagers!), and manage to virtually school our kids. We aren't preaching about virtual schooling and not living it! Like most working parents, there are days we feel overwhelmed by "doing it all" and some days we feel that we are letting our kids and families down with that constant jugging act. We also realize we have some advantages you might not as you begin to explore virtual schooling. However, we explored different approaches to education for our children, taking a leap of faith in our abilities and our kids' passion for learning. And in Lisa's case, even focusing her professional career to advocate for, develop, and manage virtual schools. Our virtual school maxim is to do our best every day, and if we don't some days, we start over the next. We aren't perfect and neither are our children. We love our children and want the best for them. Sound like someone you know? The rest you'll figure out as you go. So, let's get started!

FACTS ON VIRTUAL SCHOOLING

Virtual learning is not only here to stay, but is growing in influence and popularity daily. The International Association for K–12 Online Learning (iNACOL) is a nonprofit organization that supports access to high-quality online learning and serves as a leader in the online community. It provides resources and opportunities that allow the online community to learn, grow, and develop best practices. Recently, iNACOL published some fast facts regarding K–12 online learning and virtual schools, which can also be found on their website at www.inacol.org.

- K–12 online learning is a new field and growing at an estimated annual pace of 30 percent annually.[2]
- 42 states have significant supplemental online learning programs, or significant full-time programs (in which students take most or all of their courses online), or both. Only eight states do not have either of these options, and several of these states have begun planning for online learning development.[3]
- There are 34 state-wide or state-led virtual schools in the United States.[4]
- As of January 2007, there were 173 virtual charter schools serving 92,235 students in 18 states.[5]
- In 2000, there were 40,000–50,000 enrollments in K–12 online education.[6]
- In 2005, the Peak Group estimated online enrollments of 500,000.
- In 2006, the Sloan Consortium reported 700,000 enrollments in K–12 online learning.
- The Peak Group estimates 1 million enrollments in 2007.
- In April 2006, Michigan became the first state to require online learning for high school graduation.

The Pew Internet Project reports "the Internet is an important element in the overall educational experience of many teenagers"[7]:

- 87 percent of all youths between the ages of 12 and 17 use the Internet (21 million people).
- 86 percent of teens, 88 percent of online teens, and 80 percent of all parents believe that the Internet helps teenagers to do better in school.

- 85 percent of 17-year-olds have gone online to get information about a college, university, or other school they were thinking about attending.

Virtual schooling is access to knowledge, whether in the form of formal classes conducted in real time or recorded to be used in one's own time frame.

Virtual schooling is access to informal research, allowing a student to dive into the depths of a subject, driven by an internal passion that creates the desire to know more.

Virtual schooling is access to electronic communication that puts your child in touch with anyone anywhere in the world willing to engage in an exchange of ideas and, often, a lifetime of learning. It allows access to a globe teeming with mentors.

Virtual schooling is access to learning anywhere via technology, whether in a local park or around the world while practicing to become a Wimbledon tennis champion.

Virtual schooling is access to learning at any time via technology, allowing your child to seamlessly weave learning into the flow of life where learning styles can be honored, natural intelligences nurtured, curiosity satiated, and passions pursued.

Virtual schooling is a tool to raise your child to be a self-directed learner, a critical and lifelong skill essential for success.

Virtual schooling is a glimpse of the world your children will walk in as adults, allowing you to best prepare them to live, work, and play in a technology-centric world.

MOBILE SCHOOLING

Personal digital devices such as iPhones, iPods, and other smart phones are increasingly becoming the access point for learning. More than two thirds of children in the United States between the ages of 13 and 17 own a mobile device that they use for listening to music, texting friends and family, and communication. Optimizing our children's use of personal digital devices to include mobile learning applications can open the door so that learning can happen anywhere and anytime. It is a powerful supplemental learning tool for all approaches to virtual schooling.

Please see Chapter 8 for a list of Mobile Schooling resources.

CHAPTER 2

WHAT IS VIRTUAL SCHOOLING AND HOW DOES IT WORK?

In Chapter 1, you got a glimpse of a day-in-the life of the Kanna girls. While their education is a composite of public school programs, supplemental programs, online courses, a hybrid academy, and college classes, they are *virtual schoolers*. And just like Rebekah Gillis, who blended her high-school education by staying enrolled in her traditional high school for some courses and completing others online.

Their parents have discovered the power of *access*. Virtual schooling gives each girl access to massive resources from around the world as well as access to innovative programs in far-away school districts. Virtual schooling helps them discover and nurture their unique potentials by harnessing the power of many institutions.

We know we don't have to sell you on the notion of improving your child's education. But in an age of spending slashes at public schools across the country, how does the average citizen with limited resources achieve all this? We know that it sounds like a daunting undertaking. This book is here to show you how the same opportunity is yours for the taking.

You don't have to be a Google engineer, have a master's degree in online education, or have the patience of Job, either. Here is what you do need: The combination of your love for your child, the passion for helping them create the best future possible for themselves, and a skill you already have—being an informed and discriminating consumer. In this chapter we will explore the many methods available to harness the power of virtual schooling for your child.

SHOPPING FOR THE BEST EDUCATION

Virtual schooling is as much a new approach to education as online shopping has been to commerce. Think of virtual schooling as a tool to empower you to act as a consumer of education, encouraging competition between educational programs and schools, both real time and online, to serve up the best program for your child's needs. As your child grows, you will be helping her learn how to be a discriminating consumer.

In order to be a smart shopper, you need to know what you really need, what's available, how much it costs, and how to compare what's being offered to you. Virtual schooling is a revolutionary tool in education, which for the first time gives you, the parent, the true power of educational choice. Whether you are looking for a full-time, supplemental, or a traditional site-based school, or a combination of these—a hybrid school—the choice is yours. Your goal is to advocate, access, and always use the programs and schools that work best for your child.

COMMON VIRTUAL SCHOOLING METHODS

Virtual schooling has many incarnations and can be used in countless ways. It also is a highly dynamic education revolution, changing daily with no universal definitions or classifications. To that end, not all options are available in all states, and the same options may be referred to by many different names. Confused? Don't be. Read on and you'll be amazed at how many powerful options are available—regardless of what they might be called in your community, school district, or state.

We will be discussing the top seven approaches to virtual schooling in this chapter. In addition to learning of the benefits and challenges, you will hear from the voices of experience—families who have chosen each approach will discuss how it worked for them.

- Approach 1—Personalized learning charter school
- Approach 2—Public virtual charter school
- Approach 3—Local school or district program
- Approach 4—Going independent
- Approach 5—Supplemental programs
- Approach 6—Private online high schools
- Approach 7—The best of both worlds: hybrid or blended education

GETTING YOUR CHILD ON THE ROAD TO VIRTUAL LEARNING

You are intrigued and you want to know more. At this stage, many parents are asking themselves questions such as: How do I find the best program to meet my child's needs and my family's resources? What do all the terms mean? Do I have to be a computer genius to offer virtual schooling to my child? What if my child has special needs?

In this chapter, we will focus on creating a roadmap for you to follow to learn more and make educated decisions on the best personalized learning program for your child.

DO YOUR RESEARCH

Fortunately, there are many programs offering dynamic e-learning experiences. You should start by becoming familiar with the different types of programs and definitions so that you understand the components, expectations, challenges, and opportunities of each program and can find the best fit for your child. The first step in doing your research is to learn the terms. The information contained in this chapter will help you to safely navigate the exploratory stages of discovering which program works best for your child. What does it mean when a class is conducted "synchronously"? How is a virtual classroom different than a cyber school? What is the difference between a "supplemental" and a "full-time" program? Read on to discover the meaning of the terms and empower yourself to search without fear. Armed with your newfound knowledge, ask yourself the basic questions provided below. Create a matrix to compile and analyze your findings. Interview perspective programs and measure them against your unique needs, challenges, and desires for your child's education.

LEARN THE TERMS

Correspondence course—In this model, the instructor and student are generally not in the same physical classroom together. Electronic communication is not used. Work is submitted by hardcopy and mailed back and forth between the student and the teacher. Communication is in the form of written comments, generally on the graded work. This is the "old-school" way of distance learning prior to the Internet.

Distance learning—In this model, classes may contain no e-learning, are facilitated primarily by the correspondence method, and require some "real-time" instruction. The real-time instruction takes on many forms. The courses are completed utilizing a combination of strategies, including week-long intensive face-to-face classes, group learning, and 90 percent correspondence by regular mail with printed copies of completed work.

E-learning, online learning—This model is basically distance learning that involves the use of a computer and the Internet.

Public virtual school—This is a full-time, online, diploma-granting educational institution offering a comprehensive course catalog aligned with state standards, where students are taught directly by state-credentialed and highly qualified instructors. The school uses a combination of synchronous and asynchronous instructional techniques. There is no tuition, as it is a public school, but there can be age and geographic restrictions on enrollment. Students must participate in mandated state tests.

Private virtual school—This type of school can offer full-time or part-time enrollment depending upon the needs of the student. It is tuition-based and the fee is paid by the parent. Courses are often supported by highly qualified, certificated teachers who are trained and passionate about helping students succeed. Because it is a private school, students are freed from the traditional school calendar and can work year round.

Supplemental virtual program—Supplemental programs offer one course at a time and are generally used to complete a course of study, "retake" a class for a better grade, recover credit at the high school level, or to take advantage of a class that is not offered in the regular or home-school setting. Supplemental programs are not diploma-granting programs and can be hosted by private companies, school districts, and state education departments.

Full-time virtual learning—This is learning that takes place exclusively using resources found on the Internet. Full-time studies could take place in a public school (no cost), private online school, or under a private brick-and-mortar school that offers an e-learning option.

Virtual classroom—This is a place for instructors and students to interact and collaborate in real time. Using webcams and class discussion features, it resembles the traditional classroom, except all participants are accessing it remotely over the Internet. Lessons can be recorded and added to an e-library to complete the learning experience. Using the archived e-library, students can access and replay the teacher's lectures as many times as necessary to master the material.

E-learning course—It's the class itself. Courses include all required concepts, are aligned to state-specific standards, and typically include an electronic textbook, course syllabus, online and offline lessons, and assessments. A course can be used in both the full-time virtual school and as a supplemental course in a virtual program.

Blended model/hybrid school—This school is a combination of virtual and site-based learning. At the high school level, students can combine the power of taking a virtual class online and "going to school" for other classes. At the elementary level, some virtual schools are offering a "community day": a classroom setting overseen by the certificated teacher, who goes over academic content, problem-solving skills, group collaboration activities, and socialization. Parents love it as (especially at the elementary level) it allows for them to have some free time!

Cyber school—This is the same as e-learning or virtual school. These words are used interchangeably and denote instruction via the Internet.

Synchronous—This means learning together in real time via the virtual classroom, webcasts, seminars, or telephone. Many virtual schools offer (and some require attendance in) a synchronous class taught online. This allows the students and teacher to engage in interactive demonstrations, lectures, one-on-one tutoring sessions, and school assemblies in which students from multiple states can attend all at once.

Asynchronous—This means working independently. A student generally studies "asynchronously"—on his own time and at his own pace.

Going independent/virtual homeschooling—This refers to a method of schooling conducted independently from any organized educational institution, usually in the home setting. The teaching adults (usually the parents) choose the curriculum, arrange for field-trips, take responsibility for legal record keeping, and organize blended learning opportunities for their children.

Software—This refers to computer programs used to deliver and facilitate online lessons.

Hardware—This is the computer itself and key parts such as the motherboard, power supply, central processing unit (CPU), monitor, keyboard, and mouse.

ASK THE BASIC QUESTIONS

What type of program will best meet your child's educational needs?

- **Full time**—for full-time virtual schooling. This can be in a virtual charter school, traditional-school independent-study program, or private school.
- **Part time**—supplemental schooling for enrichment, credit recovery, or for access to hard-to-find classes (such as AP courses).

- **Blended/hybrid**—a combination of cyber and traditional learning.

What programs are available in your area?

Once you have determined which type of program best meets the needs of your child, discover the types of schools available in your area.

- **Full-time virtual charter schools**—Virtual charter schools are public schools, so their enrollment areas are restricted. Many states offer statewide virtual academies, while others, like California, require you to live within a county served by the charter school.
- **District schools**—Many local public schools offer full-time and part-time virtual courses. Call your local high school and ask to speak to the independent study or alternative education department. Ask them what type of programs they offer, how flexible the program is, and what the enrollment requirements are.
- **Personalized learning charter schools**—These are independent study charter schools that offer virtual instruction as a choice.
- **State department of education**—Several states have virtual programs run by the department of education. These are generally supplemental programs, are tuition free, and are facilitated by credentialed teachers.
- **Private schools**—No matter where you live, private virtual high schools are available for enrollment. These are tuition-based and are paid for by the parent.
- **Supplemental programs**—You can "mix and match" by purchasing a few online courses to match traditional textbooks in your child's learning program. Supplemen-

tal programs are not schools, so the student will be receiving instruction and course credit, but no diploma.

What type of support programs are you interested in?
- **Academic**—Support programs vary depending upon the age and interest of your child. In the younger years, many parents seek opportunities for their children to get together with other kids. Whether it is in an academic or social setting, many opportunities exist. Some virtual charter schools offer a "community day" or a "day on campus" wherein students can go to a learning center site, take a class, participate in clubs, and take part in student government and drama classes. At the high school level, many junior colleges offer courses for students to complement their virtual program. Tutors are available and internships exist for students to learn vocational skills.
- **Recreational**—with the rapid increase in students choosing home education (virtual or traditional), many community services have emerged to offer opportunities for kids to play sports, learn skills, take lessons, and gather together. Check out the parks and recreation district in your area and ask what type of classes are offered for students during the day. In Santa Rosa, CA, for instance, Snoopy's Ice Arena offers ice skating lessons specifically to students who are educated at home (virtually or not). In addition to the classes, the arena has a "free skate" time every Wednesday. Kids come together and skate, hang out, and work together on lessons in the cafe, and parents gather to plan events, compare lesson plans, or just have an opportunity to talk to other parents!

- **Homeschool support groups**—Most areas have support groups offered through private schools, churches, and regional areas. These groups provide years of experience in helping families to adjust to home education, including support for practical needs; tips for success, time management, money management; and encouragement. The level of support services ranges from monthly meetings to classes, graduation ceremonies, projects, "immersion learning," and more.
- **Socialization**—Locate and identify the types of programs that are available for socialization and networking purposes. Local homeschooling support groups will offer meetings, advice, support, and group learning/socialization activities for children. As home-based learning has rapidly expanded over recent years, many community-based groups have begun to offer enrichment, tutoring, and field trips to home-educated students.

DETERMINE IF VIRTUAL LEARNING IS RIGHT FOR YOUR CHILD

Can your child demonstrate the self-discipline to learn independently?

While virtual schooling has many advantages, it is not for everyone. It requires that a student have the discipline and self-motivation to get on the computer daily, check out their lesson plans, complete the lessons (both offline and online), and not be distracted by TV, video games, cell phones, MySpace, or friends.

Is your child easily distracted, or can he focus on completing a lesson?

Just because a student has difficulty paying attention in the traditional classroom does not mean that he will struggle in the virtual classroom. Oftentimes, students will not stay focused because they are bored or the lesson in not taught in their learning style. This is particularly true of kids who are kinesthetic—hands-on—learners. Our traditional system focuses on a linguistic (language-based) system. Often, lessons are taught in lectures or by reading the material, which can be frustrating for someone who learns by doing. E-learning is a terrific solution for this child because it requires the student to read and listen but also constantly interact. Many students who were previously unsuccessful in the traditional classroom have regained their self-confidence and love for learning by having success in the e-learning courses.

How comfortable do you and/or your child feel learning from a computer?

For many families who enroll their students in a virtual school, it is their first time ever having a computer in the house! They know how to plug it in and turn it on, but from there they are lost. No worries. Computer programs and online courses are becoming so "user friendly" that even a novice can learn quickly.

You might wonder about electronic maintenance. The benefit of a full virtual school is that they usually will provide a 24/7 technical support department to help you troubleshoot even the simplest of tasks. You are not alone!

Some parents love the idea of their students becoming tech savvy and having an advantage as they enter a very tech-heavy workforce. Others, however, don't like the intrusion of technology in their living space. However, virtual learning is available on a full-range spectrum, from one course to a full-time learning load.

Do you feel comfortable with an online-textbook format?

One shift from a traditional classroom to e-learning is the use of e-books, or online textbooks. These are texts presented electronically and downloaded by the student to read. The texts are just like regular textbooks, but instead of flipping a page, the student clicks to the next page in the chapter.

There are many advantages to online textbooks—but if you have never used one before, it may take a little getting used to. Online textbooks have the ability to update the information in real time. With printed textbooks, the cycle to update is usually a minimum of seven years.

Go Green! Online texts save trees. As an electronic medium, there is no need to print texts or revisions for mass distribution.

Font size can be modified for easier reading. Especially for students with visual challenges, online texts provide a simple and easy solution while allowing the student to feel successful.

A disadvantage to online textbooks is that you can't highlight key points, make notes in the margin, or mark up the text with a pen. You can print it out and do so, but it requires access to a printer.

Some students like the feel of a "real book" and can have a difficult time adjusting to the online format. However, as computers are becoming more and more commonplace, reading from an online text a skill needed to become digitally fluent.

Are you comfortable exploring the program's website?

You can get a great sense of a program and what it has to offer by exploring the website. Most websites will include information about the key players, FAQs, enrollment information, testimonials, sample lessons, a "day in the life" schedule, and academic achievement information.

While you shouldn't be swayed by slick and fancy websites, the better the website, usually, the better the program.

CREATE A MATRIX OF INFORMATION TO COMPARE THE BENEFITS AND CHALLENGES OF EACH PROGRAM TO DETERMINE THE BEST FIT FOR YOUR FAMILY (A RESOURCE GUIDE IS PROVIDED IN CHAPTER 8)

Use the matrix below as a guide to help you organize your thoughts, information, and comments. Simply gather the information from interviews, websites, and word of mouth. Insert the data into the matrix and then evaluate the best selection for your family.

Here is a sample matrix, but you should feel free to include any additional features that you are interested in comparing.

NAME OF PROGRAM	GRADES SERVED	FULL TIME OR SUPPLE- MENTAL?	COST	BLENDED PROGRAM?	REQUIRE- MENTS	COMPUTER PROVIDED?

INTERVIEW PROSPECTIVE PROGRAMS

Most virtual providers host an 800 number staffed by enrollment counselors who can answer all your questions regarding the program.

How were you treated on the call? Did the counselors seem knowledgeable? What was the response time to your query if you left a message? Oftentimes, the response time will be indicative of the level of service you can expect once you enroll in the program.

If the program has a local office, make an appointment to see the principal or executive director. Arrive prepared with a list of questions that are important to your decision-making process. Some sample questions might include:

1. Is my child eligible to enroll in the school? (age and geographic boundaries)
2. What is required of our family if we enroll?
3. Are there any hidden costs associated with enrollment?
4. Can I use my own curriculum?
5. Can I choose curriculum from a catalog, or does the school require total use of its own curriculum?
6. How flexible is the schedule?
7. Does the school follow a traditional school calendar?
8. What if we want to go on vacation in October—is that allowed?
9. What type of enrichment programs can the school offer?
10. Is there a "day on campus" or other blended opportunities?
11. Are there fieldtrips?
12. Can students dual-enroll with another school?
13. What about special education? How are services provided?
14. Does the school provide a technology package including a computer, Internet stipend, and printer?
15. How does the school view the parent? As the primary instructor? A learning coach? A mentor?
16. What role do the certificated teachers play?
17. Can my child work at her own pace?

18. What if my child wants to complete two math courses in one year—is that allowed?

19. Is there any required volunteer time?

20. How many hours a day will my child be required to study?

21. How many hours a day will my child be on the computer?

22. Are there any socialization opportunities?

23. Does the school sponsor any clubs?

24. Is the school accredited?

25. What about standardized tests? How are they administered?

26. How much paperwork is required?

27. How often do I meet with the teacher?

28. Is there a counselor who can help my child with a graduation plan?

29. How do I know that my child will be on grade level?

30. Does the school issue report cards?

31. What support systems are available to my child? To our family?

32. Are there any parent meetings? PTA?

33. Are there any school-wide celebrations?

34. What about a graduation ceremony for seniors?

35. Is there a prom?

36. Are there online clubs, communities, chat rooms for kids?

37. What about cyber safety?

38. Does the school have a parent handbook?

When you arrive for the interview, what are your first perceptions? Does the staff appear friendly and knowledgeable? What about the physical office space—does it look safe?

Through the initial interview process, you will learn a lot about the operations of the school and whether or not your child will be viewed as a special student or a number on a roster. For some statewide virtual academies, it might be too difficult to travel to the main office. In that case, schedule a phone interview with the principal, executive director, or lead teacher.

DETERMINE THE STRUCTURE OF THE PROGRAM
Course Credits
- How does the student receive course credit?
- Is the credit transferable to other high schools?
- Do community colleges and universities accept the courses to satisfy enrollment requirements?

Technology
- What type of support is available?
- Does the tech support department have a "live" person, or is it all done via e-mail and live chat?

Instructional Delivery
- Are all the courses independent study (asynchronous), or do teachers deliver any presentations live?
- Is there a virtual classroom?
- Are the courses web-based, or simply delivered to the home on a CD?
- Are there any requirements for my student to attend synchronous (live) lessons? If so, what is the time requirement?

Cost
- Are there any costs associated with the program?
- If you choose a tuition-based program, what is the payment schedule?

- Do you have to pay all of the tuition up front, or can you make monthly payments?
- Are there scholarships available?
- What if your child doesn't finish the course—do you still have to pay?
- Are there computer leasing programs available?

Cyber Safety
- How secure is the online school?
- How does the school guarantee my child's safety while online?
- Are there training classes for staff and students to learn the appropriate online behavior code?

Once you've gathered your information, it's time to make a decision. If you agree that your family will join the ranks of those who have pursued and succeeded at virtual education, congratulations! There are still preparations you need to make and you will still have a little more work to do to get started. You will need to learn about the seven different approaches and set up a learning environment that will promote your child's achievement. In Chapter 3, you will find the final portion of the roadmap designed to complete the process and firmly establish your child on the virtual road to success.

CHAPTER 3

GETTING STARTED

Some people don't like change... children included. In a traditional setting, a campus tour and visit with the prospective principal and teacher can ease a child's fear of the unknown. As you consider changing to a virtual school, begin to build excitement in your child by giving her a virtual tour of the campus, talking to real students, and creating a classroom or study area that your child can personalize and call her own. Other people love the idea of change and have no problem trying new things, including a virtual learning program. You know your child best.

SELLING THE NEW PROGRAM TO YOUR CHILD

Don't assume your child will jump right on board and sign up for virtual school. They may be having trouble in a regular classroom but at the same time be very attached to the school and not want to leave. You will want to create excitement by showing them all the "cool" things that await them in the new school. If they are older, maybe it's you who needs the convincing! Teens are not afraid of cyber learning and often will jump at the chance to take advantage of flexible scheduling and the ability to study online.

ENGAGING YOUR CHILD

Your child's success will be largely influenced by how much they "buy in" to the program. Include them in the selection process. Frame it in such a way that they feel special and excited to have this new opportunity. Show your child the websites. Meet with other families involved in the program and allow your child to meet some prospective classmates. Ask her how she feels about virtual schooling. Of course, there are times when we, as the parents, have to make the decision for them (in the case of very young children, or those who need some concrete guidance).

Once you have decided to make the move to a virtual school program, you will want to make sure that you create a positive learning environment.

SETTING UP A DEDICATED LEARNING AREA

Students can concentrate more and stay focused when they have a dedicated learning area set up with a computer, printer, curriculum, and learning supplies. The area could be as elaborate as an entire room transformed into a classroom, or a small desk space in an office. Occasionally, students like to take a break and sit on the couch with their laptops or sit at the dining room table. But unless this is the best way your child learns, reserve this for special occasions.

Follow these simple rules to create the best space possible:

1. Consider the environment. Select a location that does not have a lot of traffic and can be shut off from the rest of the living area, such as an office, a classroom, or a spare bedroom. It's OK to have a desk in the student's bedroom as long as the dedicated study area is well defined. Be sensitive to noise and do not choose an area in which other family members are congregating or watching TV, playing video games, etc.

2. Help your student build a habit of dedicated studying. Setting daily (or hourly) goals help them to stay focused. Teach them not to talk on the phone, chat on the computer, or watch TV during their study time.

3. Make sure the area has good lighting, a desk at the right height, a chair for proper ergonomics, and good ventilation.

SET REALISTIC EXPECTATIONS AND GOALS FOR SUCCESS

A major myth of online schooling is that it is easier than traditional school. In some cases, it may even be harder! Students underestimate the time, effort, and concentration required to successfully complete an assignment or course. However, for many reasons, e-learning can be very rewarding and make all the hard work pay off. A few things to keep in mind:

SET REALISTIC EXPECTATIONS FOR DAILY WORK

Most of your time will be *focus* days—those days dedicated to completing all the lessons of the day. Each subject is generally completed unless your child wants to focus on a particular subject. For instance, if she is really loving math that day and wants to move ahead in that subject, allow her the freedom to do so! Some students can finish several lessons in one day when they are on a roll. It's OK if they don't complete every subject every day. That's the beauty of flexible scheduling. Just make sure that they are completing all the lessons by the end of the learning period. Sometimes life just gets in the way of having a full focus day. Perhaps your child is physically ill or you are returning from a camping trip and are exhausted. Many parents plan *"easier days"* when they know that there will be interruptions in the day, such as a doctor's appointment or a visit from an out-of-town grandma.

Some days the community becomes your classroom. On most *fieldtrip days* your child will not be completing lessons online, but will be exploring and investigating the world around her at a zoo, museum, library, research laboratory, or a host of other educational adventures. However, you can still complete the online lesson by simply looking for lesson objectives and meeting them while you are out in the community. When you return home, ensure that your child has grasped the concepts, and if so, mark the lesson complete.

LEAVE ADEQUATE TIME TO COMPLETE LESSONS

Understand that you will learn how much time your child requires to complete her course of study. Each child progresses at his own pace, so you will need to take some time to learn your child's requirements and plan accordingly. Some children will only need 15 minutes to complete a lesson, while another child may need 60 minutes to complete the same lesson. Honor your child's natural learning cycle by allocating and planning for the right amount of time to be dedicated to schooling on a daily basis.

ACQUIRE A COURSE SYLLABUS OR CHECK THE ONLINE SCHOOL TO SEE ALL THE LESSONS AND ESTIMATED TIME FOR COMPLETION

This will help you better adjust your schedule and plan family events.

UNDERSTAND HOW MANY LESSONS NEED TO BE COMPLETED TO SUCCESSFULLY PASS THE COURSE

Oftentimes, "enrichment" or "supplemental" lessons are included in the units to help students master material—if your student already knows the material—skip it!

Some parents (especially at the elementary level) feel like they have to complete every task within the assignment to ensure that their child has learned "it all." Don't be fooled by this. Many courses come with tasks designed for different learning styles. Requiring your child to complete all of them would only lead to frustration, boredom, and much more time spent than was necessary.

Help your child set reasonable and reachable goals. If the goals are not measurable, the child could feel overwhelmed and defeated. Instead of saying "I am going to do school today" help them to plan their time accordingly. "By 10:00 A.M., finish the English lesson." This builds a sense of accomplishment and success.

While the preparation steps are universal, your options for virtual instruction vary significantly. Luckily, different programs exist to honor the uniqueness of your child, your goals, and your family situation. We have identified seven primary approaches to participate in the world of virtual schooling. Not all approaches are available in every area throughout the United States. Educational laws vary from state to state and drive the type of programs that are offered to students and families.

APPROACH 1: PERSONALIZED LEARNING CHARTER SCHOOL: VIRTUAL AND NOT

California now has 750 charter schools, 75 alone started in the year 2008. In July 2004 the California State Senate unanimously passed State Senate Resolution 36, recognizing personalized learning as a distinct education model in California.

Horizon Charter School, started in 1993, is authorized by the California Board of Education and is the state's 15th chartered school. All coursework and classes are based on California academic standards, but created with the core value of parent engagement. Madison and McKenzie Kanna attend Horizon and, while it is not their neighborhood school (in fact it is headquartered in a different county), are students of a public school and take the same standardized tests as kids at the local brick-and-mortar school, including the California High School Exit Exam. However, there are important differences. Horizon collects average daily attendance just like a traditional public school, but allocates a portion of that state funding for instructional funds to be used by request for approved programs, educational supplies, tutoring, and special community classes based on each student's goals for the semester.

Horizon is an accredited diploma-granting entity. The supervising teacher approves and awards credits for lessons completed through online classes, college classes, hybrid school classes, tutors, and community programs. Students attend on a regular school schedule and the teacher awards the attendance credit. Monthly meetings are held in which the teacher assigns lessons, reviews completed work, and evaluates the student's academic progress. The teachers use SnapGrades, an online grade-book program, which allows parents and students instant access to grades as they are posted. Those grades are carried over to the report card created by the supervising teacher. Dual enrollment classes, such as the language arts class that Madison took at Sacramento State

University, are approved by the charter school and accepted into her permanent transcript. Horizon's personalized programs fit our definition of virtual schooling: The school makes sure that students are learning and meeting state standards, while at the same time giving them countless ways to achieve a world-class education by using a collection of resources including online courses, classroom instruction, community resources, dual enrollment, vocational ed internships, and socialization opportunities, clubs, and fieldtrips.

GETTING STARTED WITH A PERSONALIZED LEARNING CHARTER SCHOOL

1. Ask yourself if playing an active role in curriculum choices is a good fit for you. If not, some personalized learning charter schools will assign the work for your child and determine the curriculum used. However, this diminishes the power of choosing the best programs for your child's learning abilities.

2. Will you be an advocate for finding available resources for your child, such as college programs, community classes, or great online classes? The supervising teacher suggests programs, but no one knows your child better than you.

3. Is your child a self-directed learner? Especially in the high school grades, having a motivated and self-directed teen (at least most of the time!) is the key to success in this method of virtual schooling.

4. If you work outside the home even part time, virtual schooling this way is difficult. Unless a grandparent, relative, or spouse can be home to facilitate the learning in the lower grades, this approach might not be right for you.

5. Interview the supervising teacher or educational specialists the charter school assigns to you before

agreeing to work with them. Sometimes personalities clash or the teacher doesn't share your family's approach to learning. Set up a meeting right from the beginning, but also request a change of teachers if the fit isn't right.

LOOKING FOR THIS TYPE OF SCHOOL?

Seek a charter school that describes itself as an independent study, personalized learning, or non-classroom-based charter school. Independent study charter schools offer the highest degree of flexibility in the public education system, but also require more parental involvement, time, and commitment. Charter schools were designed on the premise of choice and competition with the public system. Because they are public schools, they are tuition free, but they also must abide by state regulations (but not as many as traditional brick-and-mortar schools). Personalized learning charter schools can offer the best of all worlds—teachers who partner with you in the education of your child, classes, a community of learners, and the freedom to study fully online, fully offline, or a combination of both. Depending upon the state, charter schools can be authorized by school districts, the state department of education, local universities, or even the mayor (in Indianapolis, Indiana).

PERSONALIZED LEARNING CHARTER SCHOOL RESOURCES

Since personalized learning centers are locally run, there is no national clearinghouse of listings. You will need to research the schools in your area. Recipient of the Webby Award "Best Family and Parenting Site—2007 People's Voice Award," GreatSchools (www .greatschools.net) is a good place to start. Access the website, click on the "research and compare" tab, and enter your state. A list of schools will come up in your area and will give you statistics such as the loca-

tion, grades served, student population, standardized test performance scores, parent reviews, and other anecdotal information.

There are several coalitions of personalized learning center
schools that can also be a resource for you:

- U.S. Charter Schools: www.uscharterschools.org/pub/
uscs_docs/index.htm
- APLUS+: www.theaplus.org
- CharterVoice: www.chartervoice.org

APPROACH 2: PUBLIC VIRTUAL CHARTER SCHOOLS:
PUBLIC SCHOOL AT STARBUCKS AND THE ICE-SKATING ARENA

It is 11:30 in the morning on Tuesday and Gideon is sitting at his
computer, racing to finish his online math lesson in anticipation of
his upcoming gym class. At noon he will join other kids from his
virtual charter school for a lesson from a professional ice skater at
the local ice arena. While the kids skate, the parents gather in the
stands or coffee shop to talk about everything from politics to potty
training. Over in the corner two parents are intently studying the
next day's lesson and gathering tips and tricks from each other.

In another part of town, tenth-grader Beka Gillis and her mom,
Lisa, are sipping coffee while reviewing her history lesson from the
day before. The objective of the lesson is clear—to discover and
learn about the roots of democracy in the United States. The online
lesson was 12 screens (pages) long and reads much like a textbook,
but had the advantage of interactive elements embedded in the text,
such as links to references quoted, a video, and a categorization
game. Since the material in a virtual school is Internet based, wher-
ever there is an Internet signal, school is open! Another benefit of an
online lesson is the ability to have threaded discussions with classmates, a process that is similar to writing a blog. Classmates can read

messages from their peers and respond accordingly. The threaded discussion is confidential and housed within the course itself, so only enrolled students, parents, and faculty have access. Beka and Lisa's discussion turned to their upcoming trip to Washington, D.C. and how the tours of the Smithsonian, Holocaust Museum, and the American History Museum would fulfill several lesson objectives of her history class presented online.

Stacey, another student in the virtual school, enrolled for a different reason. She had suffered from peer pressure and, as a result, struggled with issues of self-esteem. She preferred to study at home, and with the lessons presented to her in the online school, the support from her credentialed teacher provided through the school, the encouragement from her mom, and the new classmates she met online, Stacey began to flourish.

Doesn't sound very virtual, does it? All of these students were enrolled in a public virtual charter school, which allowed them to receive all the benefits of a public school, yet experience the freedom of virtual education.

Public virtual charter schools are full-time, all-inclusive diploma-granting educational institutions. They are publicly funded, so like the site-based charter school, there is no tuition and the students enjoy many benefits such as teachers, special ed services, counselors, fieldtrips, and generally they receive a computer, Internet reimbursement, and student support services. This is their full-time school. Unlike a site-based charter offering virtual classes, a full-time virtual charter has no school building and the administration offices are usually in one city while the school can serve students from throughout the state. Students from the full-time virtual schools still get together, and some schools even offer a form of the hybrid program, such as a "community day." The time requirement for you, the parent, will change throughout the years, with the most intense time being in the early elementary years. When your child is enrolled in a public virtual high school, your role becomes mentor, coach, and cheerleader. Your child will have several teachers (one for each course) and will be responsible for reporting to the teachers on a daily basis. This is a great option for students who can be self-motivated and enjoy learning online, but it has less flexibility than a site-based charter and requires more direct parental involvement. The school will use a combination of synchronous and asynchronous instructional techniques to assist the students in achieving their educational objectives. The students and teacher meet in a virtual classroom and participate in interactive demonstrations, lectures, one-on-one tutoring sessions, and national assemblies. At Insight Schools, they offer "All-School Assemblies," inviting students from across the nation enrolled in virtual schools to meet and listen to world-class guest speakers in the real-time virtual classroom. For instance, last year an Olympic athlete spoke of the value of setting goals and working hard to achieve them, and on another occasion, a Holocaust survivor spoke to the students about his experiences living in a concentration camp as a child. The live session provided the opportunity for students several thousand miles apart to meet, talk, ask questions, and learn together.

Most of the work will be done "asynchronously." Most public virtual schools operate on a traditional school calendar for attendance purposes, but students can learn 24/7 as the online school is always open!

GETTING STARTED IN PUBLIC VIRTUAL SCHOOLS

Insight Schools, Connections Academy, and K^{12}, Inc., are the nation's leaders in providing virtual public schools from the elementary to the high school level. Developed by the top experts in the country, each offers a world-class education. Each national provider has similar programs, but offers different areas of specialty. Insight Schools is focused on high school only, while both Connections Academy and K^{12}, Inc., offer grades K–12 in their online schools.

Follow the steps outlined above in researching which school would be the best fit for your family. Below we've provided some overviews, brief histories, and some tips to help you start your journey.

INSIGHT SCHOOLS

In 2005, Insight Schools (www.insightschools.net) was founded around a core set of ideas that traditional high school is not for every student and that online learning can provide an attractive and effective alternative for students looking for a different experience. Online learning, at its best, provides a communication channel—students connecting with other students—combined with a rigorous and relevant academic program. Rather than being an isolating experience, Insight provides many of the socialization benefits of traditional high school, including graduation ceremonies, a prom, clubs, student government, and the opportunity to pursue outside interests. Several students, including a snowboard champion and an elite equestrian competitor, have earned national acclaim. Not all Insight students come from an easy background. For those who have faced life challenges such as sickness, financial stress, or pregnancy, Insight has provided a positive alternative to earn a high school diploma. They are fully accredited and are tuition free. Acquired in 2006 by the Apollo Group, Inc., the parent company of the University of Phoenix, Insight enjoys the benefit of being associated with the most recognized brand in education and offering that experience to its students. From only one school in the 2006–07 school year, Insight has grown to over 11 schools in ten states within just two years. They offer over 120 courses through five different tracks of learning, from foundations to AP, and a full-service educational program with credentialed teachers, administrators, counselors, a special ed department, laptops for loan to students, and a tech support department.

Families wishing to enroll in Insight Schools can go to the website (www.insightschools.net) and click on "visit our schools." While some enrollment processes differ from state to state, generally it is a simple three-step process. Step one is to complete the "Get Started Form." This will trigger a call from an enrollment specialist to assist you through the process. Step two is to review the website, read the FAQs, and speak to a staff member if necessary to determine if the school is the right fit for you. Step three is to provide an unofficial copy of your child's transcript so that courses can be properly selected. Each state has a separate 800 number that can be found on the Insight website, or you can call 800–975–8006 for more information.

CONNECTIONS ACADEMY

After sending their daughter, Allana, to first grade already knowing her multiplication, division, subtraction, and cursive writing skills, her parents worried about her school's ability to challenge her. She set off with Louisa May Alcott's *Little Women* tucked under her arm to read if she got finished with her work early. The school recognized how advanced she was and after several months, they decided to advance her ahead one grade. It wasn't enough. Still ahead of her peers and wanting a more challenging curriculum, Allana's family found the perfect fit with Connections Academy. With a mission to create academic and emotional success, Connections Academy schools deliver top-quality, personalized education that combines certified teachers, a proven curriculum, technology tools, and community experiences to create a supportive and successful environment for children who want an individualized approach to education in partnership with charter schools, school districts, and state departments of education. In Connections Academy's unique Personalized Performance Learning approach, students use daily lesson plans and curriculum materials provided by the academy. Teachers develop a learning plan for each student, whose progress is tracked through a proprietary, web-based learning management system.

Connections Academy was incubated in the Sylvan Learning family of companies. The company began operating its first schools in two states in the fall of 2002. In September 2004, Connections Academy was sold to an investor group led by Apollo Management, LP (not to be confused with the Apollo Group, Inc., mentioned above). Since then, the company has grown dramatically in terms of both the number of students served and courses provided. It was the first national K–12 virtual public school provider to be recognized by the Commission on International and Trans-Regional Accreditation (CITA).

To get started with Connections Academy virtual school, students and their families can first go to the website (www .connectionsacademy.com) to check the availability of the program in their states as well as to explore sample lessons, watch videos about the Connections Academy experience, and see answers to frequently asked questions. For those ready to take the next step, the online application tool makes it easy to check eligibility requirements, provide necessary documents, and check enrollment status. Throughout the process, help is a phone call away at 800-382-6010.

K^{12}, INC.

Founded on the idea that all children should be able to learn without limits, K^{12} began in 2000 with the vision that the advent of the Internet would allow every child access to a world-class education. It would no longer matter where a child lived. Rooted in decades of educational research and specifically focused on unlocking the innate and unique potential in each child, K^{12} offers a rigorous academic program delivered through individualized learning approaches, exceptional and engaging content that makes learning come alive, and outstanding engagement with the support of teachers.

Designed combining beautiful and well-crafted books with online materials, K^{12} has emerged as a trendsetter in the online world of curriculum development and delivery. One of the first employees at K^{12} was the author of the series "What every [X] grader should know," which drove the development process in the integration of multimedia and cognitive sciences. The students in K^{12}'s virtual academies receive not only reading and math, but science, history, art, and music as well. History studies span the world from Stone Age to the Space Age. K^{12} distributes their teachers so they can have face-to-face meetings with their students and run field trips. This face-to-face interaction builds relationships quicker and is something the families and teachers have grown to love. K^{12} students complete their online schooling experience by using the virtual classroom for instruction and community-building activities.

It is easy to enroll in a K^{12} virtual academy. Go to www.K12.com and click on "get it now." A map of the United States will pop up and you click on your state. It will show you which options are available where you live. Once there, you register through an online portal and submit supporting documents. An enrollment counselor will call you to help you through the process. K^{12} also offers a toll-free number for more information, 866-968-7512.

APPROACH 3: LOCAL SCHOOL OR DISTRICT PROGRAM: GOING TO SCHOOL—MY WAY

Virtual schooling is also for students who don't conform to the standard teenage profile. Students who become parents during high school are one such group. Rebecca is a young woman who became pregnant in high school and chose to keep her child but did not want to leave school. Her high school offered a program that allowed young moms to come to school with their babies—but what was she going to do before she had her baby? The school offered her an alternative path—to enroll in the school's independent study program and take virtual courses at home. She stayed enrolled in the local school and completed her online courses. Today, Rebecca is a successful mother and wife and works in the community. She credits the support of the alternative education program and the flexibility of the virtual school with saving her educational career and providing a pathway for her to graduate.

Rebecca is not unique. She is among the over one million students throughout the world who are finding that the power of online courses to change their lives. School-based or district-based programs are public schools run by your local school or school district. These programs are usually designated "alternative" and can be either full or part time. Your child would enroll and be a student in the local school with all the advantages and responsibilities associated with enrollment. This is a program of the local school—not a stand-alone school like the learning center or virtual charter school. The advantage to this model is that oftentimes it will offer a "blended" model, giving your child a wide range of educational options, including virtual courses; clubs; access to sports, drama, and music programs on campus; and the ability to take onsite classes such as biology labs. The disadvantage to these programs is that usually they are not the primary program that the school or district offers so they may not receive the attention that an online charter school does.

APPROACH 4—GOING INDEPENDENT: DOING HOMESCHOOL— THE VIRTUAL WAY!

Independent virtual schooling is a form of "homeschooling" using a virtual curriculum provider that provides a virtual learning program. Parents bear the cost of purchasing the program. In a complete program, courses are offered in all core areas (science, social studies, math, and language arts as well as electives ranging from art to music to foreign languages). The student has access to their own account, where their assignments are given and progress is tracked. Since it is not a school, it is not accredited and there are no course credits given toward graduation nor do the students receive a high school diploma. Going independent provides the greatest degree of flexibility in course and lesson selection and scheduling. You will need to become familiar with the homeschooling laws in your state to make sure that you comply with the statutes.

McKenna Tucker's family chose to go independent, and it allowed her the structure and freedom to perform on Broadway at the tender age of 13. Houston Tucker, McKenna's dad, says that they opted for the K^{12}, Inc., curriculum instead of going it alone as homeschoolers because they were parents, not professional educators, and they wanted to make sure that their children received a high-quality education designed by professionals with decades of cumulative experience. They chose the private option instead of the public school option for two reasons: location and freedom. They did not live in a state in which the public charter school was offered. In addition, because McKenna's performance schedule and other family commitments included a lot of travel, they liked the flexibility of the virtual program without the obligations of following a traditional school calendar and producing required paperwork.

GETTING STARTED "GOING INDEPENDENT"

As the rate of families who homeschool continues to soar (it's estimated that over two million students are homeschooled throughout the United States), so have number of support services offered. While many homeschoolers are choosing to stay within the traditional methods of instruction, many families are venturing into cyber homeschooling. Type in "virtual homeschooling" into a search engine, and you will find a myriad of sites to help navigate the virtual waters, introduce you to support groups, offer advice, and point you in the right direction to select curriculum and supplies.

Remember—while these sites may not be specifically devoted to cyber homeschooling, many of the strategies and challenges are the same. Venture into the site Virtual Homeschool Group (www.virtualhomeschoolgroup.com) or Choosy Homeschooler (www.choosy homeschooler.com) to discover more about virtual homeschool groups and look for online tools.

Hundreds of curriculum vendors exist on the web. Look to the resource guide in Chapter 8 to get a head start. K^{12}, Inc (www.k12 .com) offers engaging and high-quality online content, and Global Student Network (www.globalstudentnetwork.com) has in-depth reviews of different courses you can purchase.

APPROACH 5—SUPPLEMENTAL PROGRAMS: JUST WANT A TASTE? TRY THIS ONLINE!

Do you want virtual enrichment? Does your child just need a few courses? Supplemental programs are intended to provide individual online instruction to students who are already receiving full-time instruction in an existing public school, private school, or homeschool environment. Supplemental programs are not diploma-granting programs and do not offer services such as special ed, but they do provide a very valuable resource for schools and parents in finding individual courses to help a student make up credits or round out an educational program. The courses are fee based, usually paid for by the school, department of education, or parent.

Offering the greatest degree of flexibility, purchasing courses independently is a big advantage to students who need to make up credits or want to access courses not available at their local high school. The Florida Virtual School (FVS) is a great example of a successful program offering supplemental education. Founded in 1997, it was the country's first statewide online high school. According to their website, last year, FVS served over 63,675 students in 137,450 half-credit enrollments. They accept students both within Florida and all over the world.

The South Carolina Virtual School Program was started in September 2007. The legislature was proactive in seeing the need to offer alternative forms of education to the students of South Carolina and passed a bill in May 2007 authorizing virtual education. The South Carolina Department of Education responded and began to offer courses to students enrolled in high schools and homeschools across the state. By February 2009, the department was overwhelmed by the response. Over 13,000 students have requested courses. Since supplemental programs are not schools, there are no support services available to students, rather the programs offer an innovative way of making more courses available than students might otherwise be able to take.

Supplemental courses are advantageous to districts as well. For example, a remote district in northern Colorado might have difficulty attracting a teacher for an AP calculus class when there are only four students who would qualify and are interested in enrolling in the course. Instead of turning the kids away, the district can purchase the supplemental course for those students and offer it without having a teacher move to the remote area.

GETTING STARTED FOR SUPPLEMENTAL EDUCATION

First, determine what your needs are. Do you want to just purchase curriculum or enroll in a school like Florida Virtual School or

Olympus High School, where you can purchase one class at a time? Call your state department of education and see if they offer a supplemental virtual program like South Carolina's. Conduct research on the web. The Internet is filled with programs, schools, and companies offering course-by-course programs. iTunes U offers many supplemental learning opportunities from some of the nation's most prestigious Universities—all free. iTunes U provides a virtual lens to learning about current events and historic legacies. Finally, access the resource guide in Chapter 8 to see a comprehensive listing of websites.

APPROACH 6—PRIVATE ONLINE HIGH SCHOOLS: SUCCESS WITHOUT STRINGS

She was gifted and talented. Her first two years of high school were filled with academic success, a spot on the school soccer team, and a place in the art honor society. But midway through her junior year, she faced unexpected health challenges. Her dad, Ed Harris, knew exactly where to turn for solutions. Ed had spent many years working both as an executive and a board member for several charter and online high schools. He knew the advantages of virtual learning and saw the opportunity for his daughter to benefit from the vast resources that were available to parents. Due to her need for rest, it was best for her to complete the lessons on her own time schedule which could be matched well with her peak times of productiveness during the day. She might begin at 1:00 P.M. and finish at 1:00 A.M. Instead of a public virtual school, they opted to enroll in a private school. They had to pay for the program, but the flexibility and ability to study at her own pace were priceless. She was granted an extension in two courses and finished just a few weeks prior to heading off to college. In the regular public school or even a virtual public school, she would not have been able to take advantage of an extension and would not have graduated in time for college. Their decision and efforts paid off. She was accepted into several highly acclaimed universities and settled on her dream school—the Maryland Institute College of Art.

Private online high schools offer the best option within a structured program for full flexibility. Private online schools provide you with high-quality curriculum, support, tutoring, and the option of full- or part-time enrollment. The biggest difference is that they are tuition based and parents pay the fee. In a private school, your child does not have to adhere to the board-adopted regular school calendar, so you have more flexibility not only in the course levels you choose, but the days of the year that you choose to conduct school. You can register anytime, and can take advantage of full-time learning, individual classes, or even dual-enrollment courses, which provide an opportunity for your child to receive college credit while still in high school.

GETTING STARTED WITH PRIVATE ONLINE HIGH SCHOOLS

As people are realizing the power of the Internet and the freedom of choice, private online high schools are becoming more prevalent. One new school to keep an eye on is Olympus High School (www .olympushighschool.net). Several high-quality private high schools exist in the marketplace. Do your research. Access each website and explore their course catalog. How many courses do they offer? Do you have to pay upfront? Is there a payment plan? Do teachers come with the courses, or is it just like buying an electronic textbook? Is the school accredited? In addition to courses and cost, investigate what type of support services the school might offer. For example, Olympus High School provides a teacher, the online school, access to 24/7 tutoring, and a school community. What type of support services does the school you are considering offer? Are there clubs? Regional events?

Some high schools, such as K^{12}, Inc., are part of a bigger virtual educational system. In addition to its public and independent schools, K^{12} offers a private high school solution called the K^{12} International Academy (www.k12.com). With the International Academy, K^{12} is purposefully trying to create a student base of kids all over the world to give them a world-class education. Keystone National High School (www.keystonehighschool.com) and Kaplan High School (www.kaplanhighschool.com) are two other good options. A comprehensive list can be found in the resource guide in Chapter 8.

The cost for a program depends on how many courses you order. If you purchase a full-time program, there is usually a discount on the complete package. Generally, you can expect to pay around $495 per course or up to $8,000 for a complete program.

APPROACH 7—THE BEST OF BOTH WORLDS—HYBRID OR BLENDED: HYBRID ISN'T ONLY FOR CARS!

Blended-model programs have received much attention lately. Touted as the "school of the future," the blended model addresses many challenges currently in the education system. It takes on many different forms, but consistently involves a blend of "face-to-face" learning opportunities (usually in a campus classroom) and virtual coursework, providing opportunities for students to receive direct instruction, collaborate with peers in the learning process, and socialize, and for parents to receive support and training.

Lisa Gillis, one of the co-authors of this book, is a pioneer in the field of blended instruction, having successfully designed and implemented blended programs that have gained statewide recognition for over ten years. She advocated for her daughter, Rebekah, to study in a blended virtual model so that they could travel together and Rebekah could enjoy the benefits of integrating real-life experiences (like sitting in a legislative committee hearing and having lunch with a senator) with the online lessons.

What do the many models of blended schools look like? Consider Chicago public schools. Under the leadership of CEO Arne Duncan (now U.S. Secretary of Education) and the Renaissance 2010 program, the district has sponsored two blended-model programs. Launched in 2006, Chicago Virtual Charter School offers a glimpse into the future. On center days (the days in which the students attend classes at a learning center), learning coaches (parents) and their students arrive at the learning center before 9:00 A.M. classes begin. The student population of nearly 600 is divided into eight different morning and afternoon sessions from Tuesday through Friday. The classes are quite small with a maximum student-to-teacher ratio of 15:1, a number large enough for group projects but small enough to allow for a great deal of teacher-student interaction. Most work is project-based and interactive. Some teachers assign homework.

Pam Cray, a homeschool veteran, teacher, and virtual-school professional, delivers a weekly training and support program for parents with students enrolled in the school. Topics vary from how to navigate the online school to how to set up a schedule that works. If the parents are unable to attend the face-to-face training sessions there are two virtual sessions offered the following Monday.

Students may get involved in student government, young authors, yearbook, book club, runners club, drama, and more. Hybrid students have classmates, teachers, lessons, a yearbook, school pictures, field trips, vision and hearing screenings, and fire drills, but they complete a majority of their lessons online at home.

Another Chicago hybrid school making some noise is the Virtual Opportunities Inside a School Environment (VOISE) Academy. This is a new twist to both the online and traditional school models.

The school distributes free laptops for use both at school and at home for homework. There are no traditional textbooks, no pencils, no chalkboards. All instruction is done on the laptop. The virtual program is blended with projects, collaborative learning opportunities, and a chance to connect with a teacher on a daily basis. Students have a full course catalog of virtual classes available to them—much more than would be available in a traditional school. As an all-digital, in-person school environment, VOISE has captured the attention of the nation and many will continue to watch its progress.

In 2005, California Virtual Academies (CAVA) piloted a hybrid program in one site in Santa Rosa, serving 100 students one day a week. Parents could stay for the parent program or drop off their kids and have some free time. By 2006, the program had expanded to eight sites and served over 800 students. Many parents felt that the hybrid program was an optimum combination of virtual education and the socialization provided in the traditional schoolhouse model. Lorie Florence found the answer to her child's educational needs by enrolling in the Community Day program sponsored by CAVA. As a credentialed teacher, she had many years of experience in public schools, charter schools, and with homeschooling. But she still had trouble getting her children to listen when it came to schoolwork. Reporting to a computer helped take the "mom" out of home education. The teacher and online lesson provided another "authority" from which her child could learn—a partner in the educational process.

At CAVA's Community Day, credentialed teachers taught the state standards and checked in with the parents about things they noticed, like a pencil incorrectly held, or a tendency to squint, or big things like being behind in math skills. Students learned how to line up, raise their hands, and ask to go to the bathroom. This program proved that enrolling in a "virtual" world doesn't mean that you have to give up on "real" relationships.

Many experts believe hybrid or blended schools will eventually replace traditional schools. Some virtual schools like Insight School of Kansas are offering a vocational training component by partnering with a local construction company to allow students to gain workforce skills while earning their high school diploma.

Virtual schooling is about accessing the best, most innovative virtual and real-time learning programs and resources and matching them with what your child needs to build a successful future. Regardless of the approach you choose, your child's experience will vary according to her development and maturity. Her social and academic needs will vary from elementary to middle to her high school years. In the following chapters, we will explore what virtual learning looks like during those crucial years and how you can maximize her education to accommodate and honor her growth.

CHAPTER 4

PERSONALIZED LEARNING: GETTING TO KNOW YOUR UNIQUE LEARNER

"*T*here is no one alive who is Youer than You.*" This is a wonderful quote from Dr. Seuss that reveals the essence of children—they are who they are who they are. Parents of more than one child know this well—even though we feel that we've raised each child with the same parenting style, each grows into an individual filled with a unique combination of gifts, talents, personality types, and learning styles. As a loving parent, there is no one alive who knows your child more thoroughly than you, and there is no one more passionate about helping her reach her full potential. Each child deserves a customized education within the context of exploring his world and his potential.

In this chapter, we will explore personalized learning, which is the foundation for a successful virtual school experience. It is a way of learning that combines learning styles, intelligences, personality traits, passion-based learning, and the learning environment into one educational experience for your child.

While we are not professional psychiatrists, we are experienced parents, virtual schoolers, and classroom teachers (including teaching and educational therapist certifications). This background has given us the experience to teach you how to put together the puzzle pieces that make up a successful personalized learning experience. Some of the information will be familiar to you, while other components might be new, so we encourage you to explore the books and resources within each section.

When an educational approach is aligned with a child's dominant intelligences and aptitudes, it is easy for that child to stay motivated. A child that is nurtured to respect the pace at which he or she likes to learn, as well as her intelligences, unique talents, and passions, will learn to respect them. Getting to really know your children will ensure they'll discover who they are.

CREATING A PERSONALIZED FRAMEWORK FOR VIRTUAL LEARNING

We will learn how to identify the key puzzle pieces of learning styles, intelligences, personality types, the pursuit of passions, and environments so that you can create a dynamic and relative learning program for your child.

PUZZLE PIECE 1: LEARNING STYLES

When Harry Potter first became the world's favorite wizard, Jordan, age ten, was only reading books that were assigned to him in school. His mother picked up the CD set of *The Sorcerer's Stone.* Then a magical thing happened: Jordan became a reader. His love of reading was ignited not just by a great story, but by a story delivered to him in *his* learning style: Jordan is an auditory learner. He learns best by *listening*.

Listening is a way of absorbing information. It is one of the three styles of taking in information: **visual**, when a child learns best by seeing; **auditory**, when a child learns best by listening and speaking; and **kinesthetic**, when a child learns best by doing (also called hands-on learning). Every child, yours included, has a preferred learning style. By studying your child's learning habits, you may already suspect or know how your child learns best.

Does your son love to tell you stories about his day in great detail? He could be an auditory learner. Does your daughter build huge Lego castles and have to touch everything to learn how to use it? She could be a kinesthetic learner. When our children are toddlers, it appears as though they are all kinesthetic learners as they explore and touch everything. However, as they grow, with careful observation, you'll be able to determine their inborn learning style. Oftentimes, you can determine a child's learning style by observing her first movements in the process she goes through to learn something that interests her. While you can't tailor every learning experience to your children's learning style, just being aware of it and teaching them how they learn best allows you (and them!) to look for different technology and delivery methods of education that respect that style.

In traditional schools, most instruction is delivered for the "linguistic" (reading and writing) and the mathematical-based learner. A kinesthetic learner with a short attention span, on the other hand, will want to get up and go. They'll want to learn how a simple machine works by taking the motor apart and figuring out how all the pieces go back together again. Within five minutes, the kinesthetic learner disengages, gets bored and frustrated, and tunes out from a purely auditory presentation.

Respecting Learning Styles in Virtual Schooling

By accessing a well-crafted lesson online, a child is learning with a personalized approach—receiving information suited to his or her learning style. If your child struggles with traditional schoolwork, you can help him master the information by finding it presented in a different way. Your child can click on the lesson about simple machines and watch an animated motion picture. Throughout the lesson, children can be encouraged to interact by clicking on different components, building virtual machines, and watching them perform (or blow up). They can see videos of top-performance machines. They can listen to interviews. They can even play simulated games to master the concepts.

If you are looking to supplement your child's traditional school education, download lectures from iTunes U for your auditory learner. They can also watch online videos or DVDs to gain knowledge of an interest or subject.

Great Resources for Uncovering Your Child's Learning Style
- *In Their Own Way: Discovering and Encouraging Your Child's Multiple Intelligences (Revised and Updated)*, by Thomas Armstrong
- *Coloring Outside the Lines: Raising a Smarter Kid by Breaking All the Rules*, by Robert Shank
- Learning styles assessment online: www.aselfportrait online.net/store/CustomerReg.asp

What Is Your Learning Style?

As parents, we often have trouble understanding our children and their unique learning style. Because we are unique human beings with dominant learning styles, we view the world through that lens. If we are good readers, we don't understand that reading doesn't come easily to everyone. If we can capture a lecture better by listening and not taking notes, it is hard to fathom anyone not under-standing the spoken word. It is critical that you understand your own learning style so that you can discover the difference in your child's innate ability to learn. Oftentimes, your child will have a different style of learning than you. If you are linguistic learner, you will want to "read everything." If your child doesn't like reading or is more interested in learning how a simple machine works by taking it apart rather than reading the instructions, this could cause friction in your home. Frustration results when a parent or teacher with a different learning style expects a child to learn not in the child's unique learning style, but in the parent's learning style. Understand that all people learn differently and give your child the room to learn in his unique style.

This is important in the virtual world because it will help determine the type of lessons you choose, the length of each lesson, and how to adapt the online content to project-based learning, as well as the kind of learning space you create for your child.

Learning Styles Resources

Several websites offer learning styles assessments. Some are free, and some charge a modest amount to take and interpret the results (about $5.00 per person). If you are interested in finding out more, you can explore the following websites:

- www.learningstyles.net
- www.ldpride.net/learningstyles.MI.htm
- www.VARK-Learn.com

PUZZLE PIECE 2: MULTIPLE INTELLIGENCES

Intelligence changes and expands throughout life. Education expert Howard Gardner of Harvard University has identified eight intelligences (www.howardgardner.com). The combination of these eight intelligences makes up our intellect, an elegant mix as unique as our fingerprints.

Our children are explorers in their early years, and they may exhibit preferences or strengths in one particular intelligence but then move to another. *Since your child's intellect is growing daily and is a combination of all the intelligences in various degrees, be careful not to "box" your child into one or two intelligences.* It is key to find the best learning resources—both virtual and real-time—with which to stimulate their intelligences.

Don't confuse intelligence with performance on IQ tests. We are talking about intelligence as the natural way your child (and you!) approaches learning and problem solving. IQ tests (and other standardized intelligence tests) measure brain function and the ability to solve, analyze, interpret, and predict information based upon presented facts and rank the score against a predictor scale. On the other hand, the eight intelligences identified by Gardner help us understand the way we learn and our natural gifting. Your child will be most successful and joyful when they are learning in a style that complements, not conflicts with, their natural intelligence. Not all intelligences can be nurtured with online programs.

AN OVERVIEW OF GARDNER'S EIGHT INTELLIGENCES

1. **Linguistic intelligence:** language-based learning
2. **Logical-mathematical intelligence:** concrete, sequential learning
3. **Musical intelligence:** learning through music
4. **Bodily-kinesthetic intelligence:** learning by doing (hands-on)
5. **Spatial intelligence:** learning through understanding spatial relationships
6. **Interpersonal intelligence:** learning through the strong ability to relate to others

7. **Intrapersonal intelligence:** learning through the ability to explore one's emotions
8. **Naturalist intelligence:** learning through nature and the environment

Applying Multiple Intelligences to Virtual Schooling

After you've identified your child's strongest or emerging intelligences, look for ways to stimulate them both online and with real-time learning projects. Incorporate projects and activities into your child's virtual learning program that respect her unique learning style and intelligences. Projects can include: contributing to discussions in the virtual classrooms, suggesting the formation of new clubs, signing up for committees, and utilizing online social networking tools. Take advantage of opportunities for "real-life" learning with other kids in a community day or co-op, stay involved in sports teams and recreation classes, volunteer in the community, conduct hands-on science experiments, build models, create art projects, and learn music.

Realize that one size does not fit all and just like traditional school isn't for every child, the virtual school is not for every child, either. Make sure that your child will feel comfortable studying and learning in a high-tech environment. More on educational programs can be found in Chapters 5 and 6.

Resources on Intelligences

- *Multiple Intelligences: New Horizons in Theory and Practice,* by Howard Gardner
- *Five Minds for the Future,* by Howard Gardner
- *In Their Own Way: Discovering and Encouraging Your Child's Multiple Intelligences (Revised and Updated),* by Thomas Armstrong

PUZZLE PIECE 3: PERSONALITY TYPES

Each person is born with his own unique personality type. Some children are introverts (shy) while others are extroverts (outgoing). Different theories have identified up to 16 different personality types, but there are four types that can be generally agreed upon:

Yellow type: happy-go-lucky, optimistic, outgoing, glass is always half full, anything is possible. This child lights up the room by simply walking in. They are often seen as a ray of sunshine—always smiling, happy, and positive. These children will seek leadership roles, acting, or anything that allows them to be center stage (extrovert).

Red type: loud, outgoing, take-charge, dominant. This child will always want to be in charge (extrovert).

Blue type: quiet, introverted, deep, introspective. These children like to write, reflect, compose music, and connect to others at a deep, personal level (introvert).

Green type: conciliatory, easygoing, usually introverted. These children hate conflict and will play the peacemaker and even forfeit their needs or desires in an attempt to bring a solution to a problem. They have a high need for approval (introvert).

Applying Personality Types to Virtual Schooling

If your child is more introverted, she will probably be quite satisfied with learning from a computer-based program. In fact, removing her from the constant stress of a people-packed environment can be a relief. Give her room and space to think deeply and take as much time as she wants in researching, analyzing, and making deep connections.

If your child is more extroverted, she will want to use the computer as a foundational tool, but will need her "people fix." Look for programs or classes that allow her to interact with other students. In the virtual environment, she will want to participate in the monitored chat rooms. Even in the virtual classroom, she will be the first to want to raise her hand and volunteer her thoughts. Give her ample opportunities to take leadership roles. If a student government doesn't exist in her school, she can help start one. Clubs and extracurricular activities are especially important to her, so make sure that she can stay focused long enough on her studies to take part in the "fun stuff."

PUZZLE PIECE 4: THE PURSUIT OF PASSION

Few can deny that Steven Spielberg is a movie-making genius. How did his parents help him discover and hone that genius? Where did that talent and passion for film-making come from? It came from working toward earning a Boy Scout merit badge in photography. We aren't kidding.

After fulfilling a requirement for a merit badge by making a nine-minute 8 mm film, Spielberg's parents recognized his interest and passion for making movies and bought him a Super 8 Kodak movie camera. When Steven wanted to shoot a space scene, his mother took him to the desert to film on location. His family dressed up in costumes and starred in the movies. Leah Spielberg was not a parent that told her son to "go outside and play." She nurtured his passion for film-making, even when it wasn't easy to do so. She advocated for him, getting a hospital to shut down an entire wing when he needed to film a scene. She helped him by making costumes, and actually put the letters in the marquee when at 14 he debuted his first sci-fi flick, *Firelight,* at a theater in Phoenix. (The movie was actually profitable!)

When Steven needed to shoot a bloody horror scene she went to the supermarket and bought 30 cans of cherries, which she cooked in a pressure cooker until they exploded all over the room. "For years after that," she jokes, my routine every morning was to go downstairs, put the coffee on, and wipe cherry residue off the cabinets."

What is your child passionate about in and outside of school? What interests are they developing? Transforming your child's education into virtual schooling requires that you be on the lookout for those first signs of interest of what could become his life's work. As a parent today, you have many more resources at your fingertips to help your child explore a particular interest, curiosity, or passion. How many passions or interests in childhood are ignored or never see the light of day?

In 2005, Yahoo! HotJobs conducted extensive job seeker research. According to the results, more than three out of four Americans (78 percent) believe there is a dream job out there for them . . . yet less than a third believes their current job is "the one."

The purpose of our children's education is to prepare them for adulthood, not just to take tests to move on to the next grade. Where they will end up is determined in large part by how they explore their passions and the belief that being passionate about their work, interests, and life is important.

Applying Passion to Virtual Learning

Allow your child to explore different topics on the Internet. What is it that she wants to learn more about? If she could write a research report on any topic, what would she choose? Her answer will give you a clue to her passion. If her passion is knowledge—perfect! What better instrument for discovering knowledge than a virtual program. Is her passion acting? Download acting lessons from the Internet and complement that by enrolling her in a local drama class that culminates in a live performance. Is his passion video games? Find a virtual school that offers game design and allow him to take it for credit in high school. You get the idea. The virtual environment can be adapted to accommodate any passion. But there is one thing the virtual school cannot do—it cannot discover your child's passion for you. That is your privilege.

PUZZLE PIECE 5: ENVIRONMENT

What type of environment do you offer your child? Do you value education and see each opportunity as a "teachable moment"? Are you organized? Do you allow them the freedom for self-discovery and involve them in the decision-making process regarding their education?

Your child will thrive in an environment in which they feel safe, protected, and supported. Children learn by observing. Are there books scattered throughout the home? Do you have probing conversations about current events at the dinner table? Are they taught the value of serving others by providing opportunities to take a meal to a sick neighbor or volunteer at the food pantry? In addition to providing a positive study environment, provide a mental environment that encourages exploration, discovery, and the room to take risks.

Applying the Environment to Virtual Learning: Learning to study at their own space, place, and pace.

Throughout this book, we offer suggestions on how to model appropriate learning behavior to your children and set up an environment for success. Choose a learning program that doesn't hinder them, but rather promotes their ability to study at their own space, place, and pace. Engage in the learning process with your child. Teach them, talk to them, question them, and listen to them.

PUZZLE PIECE 6: NATURAL INSTINCTS

Kathy Kolbe was the first to identify four universal human instincts used in creative problem solving. She believes that your child was born with instincts that follow an innate pattern. These patterns determine your child's unique mode of operation. These instincts are not measurable. However, the observable acts derived from them can be identified and quantified by the Kolbe A™ Index. These instinct-driven behaviors are represented in the four Kolbe Action

Modes: **Fact Finder**—the instinctive way we gather and share information; **Follow Thru**—the instinctive way we arrange and design; **Quick Start**—the instinctive way we deal with risk and uncertainty; and **Implementor**—the instinctive way we handle space and tangibles.

According to Kolbe: "When people act according to instinct, their energy is almost inexhaustible—like water running downhill. But when people are forced to act against their instinct, their energy is rapidly depleted—like water being pumped uphill."

There are two Kolbe Indexes that can identify the natural way your youngster takes action. The Kolbe Y™ Index is designed for children with a fourth-grade reading level to 17 years old. The Kolbe IF™ for Kids Index is completed by a parent or adult observer of children from the ages of two to eight. To learn how to translate your child's unique natural instincts and gain more detailed information on the four Kolbe Action Modes, we recommended you take the time to learn more about the Kolbe Index at www.kolbe.com, or even better, take the Kolbe Index yourself and find out where your unique genius lies. Then, do the same for your child.

MATH SUCKS! THE POWER OF PERSONALIZED VIRTUAL LEARNING IN ACTION

Okay, so your daughters just declared that they are never going back to their algebra class because "math sucks, Mom!" What do you do when your children don't *like* algebra? It takes more work to keep children inspired and interested in a subject when it isn't something they are passionate about or have a natural aptitude for. Here is where personalized learning and the power of virtual education really packs a punch to keep your child engaged and enthused about learning even though the required subject they must master is a struggle for a myriad of reasons. While writing this book, both co-authors Elizabeth and Lisa experienced this in their personal lives. As McKenzie Kanna was struggling in her pre-algebra class in her hybrid school, which has a strong emphasis on engineering, math, and science, Rebekah Gillis was tuning out of her algebra 2 class taught through a method involving more discovery and group learning than direct instruction. The two girls had different but similar stories and their moms were intrigued as they found themselves discussing how to best support their children. The solution that both Elizabeth and Lisa chose? Virtual schooling for math. Kenzie doesn't have a passion for math and does not have a strong aptitude for it. Nonetheless, she must master the subject to move on to state-required math courses. Both Elizabeth and Lisa took action. They followed the simple five-step process outlined below to bring learning home for their daughters.

STEP 1: CREATE A PLAN

Kenzie took a pre-algebra assessment online at www.letsgolearn.com to identify which concepts she was struggling with. This would help to determine the best collection of instructional materials to specifically address her needs. From the review, focus areas were identified and a plan was constructed for Kenzie's tutor and her parents to work with her.

STEP 2: IDENTIFY THE PUZZLE PIECE OF LEARNING STYLES

Kenzie is an auditory learner. She sings songs, hums, has an innate talent at mimicking just about anything she hears. Elizabeth downloaded some podcasts on algebra at iTunes U for her to listen to. Additionally, as an auditory learner, Kenzie does well having her lessons explained at her own pace, thus a tutor is perfect for her. Although the hybrid school has a great pre-algebra class, it is not at Kenzie's pace.

STEP 3: IDENTIFY THE PUZZLE PIECE OF HER DOMINANT INTELLIGENCE

As a digital native, like all children, Kenzie loves playing computer games. Elizabeth purchased *Math Blasters Pre-Algebra* and *Math for the Real World* CDs. While not as alluring as the latest version of Kenzie's favorite software game, *Nancy Drew,* computer games are a great way to help a child shore up areas they are struggling with in school. Kenzie has a strong linguistic intelligence, which means she is "word smart" and likes to read.

STEP 4: CREATE A POSITIVE LEARNING ENVIRONMENT

Her mom picked up a couple of great books written by *The Wonder Years* actress Danica McKellar: *Kiss My Math: Showing Pre-Algebra Who's Boss* and *Math Doesn't Suck.* Kenzie loves these books and has read them several times. They are engaging and she has an affinity for them. They are written in language teenage girls speak: "I'm sorry, but 'integer' has got to be the most boring, sterile word I've ever heard. Doesn't it remind you of some type of medical instrument used in a hospital?"

STEP 5: FIT ALL THE PIECES TOGETHER

By doing your research and finding products or learning resources in your child's learning style, you can transform a subject from one endures to one enjoys. Kenzie is also learning something other than pre-algebra in the process. She is learning how to access resources tailored to her learning style and personality.

A DIFFERENT APPROACH

One size does not fit all—even in the virtual learning world! As Elizabeth and Lisa discovered, they both arrived at the same solution—virtual learning—but approached it differently.

Rebekah was an honors student who had always enjoyed math. In fact, in elementary school, she was dubbed the "Math Queen." During her first two years in high school, she enjoyed and looked forward to math class. A's were the norm for her. That all changed her junior year. With a different instructional method and difficult subject matter, she was not grasping the concepts in algebra 2. When Beka got her first failing grade on a midterm exam and tutoring was not helping, Lisa began to investigate her options. She elected to enroll Beka in a private online high school to take a supplemental course so that she could progress at her own pace.

It was not the easiest transition, because it required Beka to be a much more self-directed learner. However, once she learned how to navigate around the online school, she has soared and is back on track. She finished her first semester earning an A in the class and even completed some units with a perfect 100% score!

We covered getting to know your child, his learning styles, intelligences, personality, passions, natural instincts, environments, and love of learning. Learning how to create a personalized virtual learning program will provide the strongest foundation for success. We are confident that as you begin to understand the pieces of the puzzle that must fit together for the best educational experience, your child will emerge as the masterpiece you are laboring so hard to create.

In the following chapters, we will explore the specifics of virtual learning at both the elementary and high school levels to better equip you to create a personalized virtual learning plan for your child.

Learning styles are how your child *takes in* information, and he or she is born with them. Intelligences are what he or she *knows*. Intelligences, like knowledge, change and expand throughout life.

Children have several potentials—not just one potential, as is often incorrectly stated. The definition of potential is expressing possibility. Does your child have one possibility for success in life? Of course not. For example, if your child has a talent for art, does that mean she only has a potential to be an artist? Uncovering your child's potential in a sport does not mean that is the *only* special talent he has to expand and grow. Just as life holds several opportunities and possible life paths, your child has many hidden potentials just waiting for you to nurture. Think of the word "potential" as a verb. Think of your child's potentials as always in motion and *possible*.

CHAPTER 5

VIRTUAL SCHOOLING AND THE ELEMENTARY YEARS

One of the first questions parents ask when considering virtual schooling for their young child is, "How many hours will my child need to spend in front of a computer?"

While some computer geeks (such as Bill Gates and Steve Jobs, and the founders of Google, Larry Page and Sergey Brin), have done very well as adults, the idea of our six-year-old staring at a monitor six to eight hours a day strikes parents as an unappealing prospect. Rest assured, even if you enroll your child in a full-time virtual school program the amount of time they'll spend using a computer is directly correlated to their grade level.

One of the greatest myths about virtual education is that kids spend their days in front of a computer. In reality, at the kindergarten level, the time they spend at a computer is about 35 minutes a day. Increase that to around three hours a day by the eighth-grade level and maybe a little more during high school, depending upon their assignments and research projects.

Some parents express concern that too much screen time might damage their children's eyes. According to the American Optometric Association, there is no conclusive research that long-term use of computer video display terminals is harmful to the eyes. Most eye strain is caused by poor lighting or the improper placement of the reading supplies, computer screen, or keyboard. Children often have a limited degree of self-awareness, so they may get wrapped up in a project on the computer and not realize they haven't taken time to rest their eyes. Pacing, awareness, and taking breaks are the best ways to prevent eye strain when learning online.

It is likely that computer time won't be a problem for your child at all. Baby boomers may be wary of computers and digital media, but a young child today has grown up in a digital world. From satellite TV to cells phones, iPods, GPSs, and text messaging—kids know how to communicate using technology. It's only natural for this process to permeate education as well. The child who masters technology now will find himself better equipped for mastering the world in the future.

While it seems in some ways that technology and computers have been a part of our lives for some time, less than just ten years ago, few could have envisioned an elementary school completely online. One night while helping his young daughter with her homework, Ron Packard, founder and CEO of K^{12}, Inc, had a vision of an elementary school with no doors—it was never closed, and any child could attend. Packard's vision of this futurist school included offering the knowledge of the core skills every elementary school–age child needs to learn. These futurist virtual schools are revolutionary, but the fundamentals they are built on are based on years of research regarding how your child learns. The first four years (K–3) are spent mastering basic skills. The next four years (4–8) are spent using the skills to build knowledge. The last four years (9–12) are spent using the knowledge to build wisdom and applications to the real world.

We will be explaining the different roles of the student, parent, and teacher within virtual education. As an example, we have chosen to focus on the kindergarten year, as most of the core principles remain the same throughout the elementary years of education.

THE ROLES OF STUDENT, PARENT, AND TEACHER IN VIRTUAL SCHOOLING

The best educational program for your child will be a combination of different "systems" (parents, student, teacher, learning program) working together.

PARENT'S ROLE

The early elementary years will require a lot of focus and time. You can expect your child to be engaged in learning activities for two to three hours a day at the kindergarten level and build up to five to six hours a day at the third-grade level. You will need to be physically present on a daily basis to plan the lessons, gather the instructional materials, arrange for play dates, take part in a support group, and assist your child daily with the lessons. One of the benefits of joining a structured virtual school program is that all of the lessons have been designed for you. The virtual public school offers the curriculum and provides a teacher to help you along the way. However, the public school does come with more restrictions than cyber homeschooling or "going independent." Because of the pressure to be tested and "check off the boxes" some parents prefer the freedom of going totally independent or using virtual schooling to supplement their child's education.

STUDENT'S ROLE

During the kindergarten year, your child will learn how to see a task to completion. After years of free playtime, her attention span is not developed and she may jump from one activity to the next. You will need to teach her the value of staying on task until the lesson is finished.

The average day for a kindergartner is between two and three hours of instruction. The day is filled with an assortment of learning activities, from accessing the online school (about 35 minutes of computer time per day) to completing hands-on projects, workbooks, and basic science experiments—not to mention frequent breaks to exercise and participate in exploratory play (like putting together Lego's, playing house, completing puzzles, etc.).

TEACHER'S ROLE

Depending upon the type of school you choose, the role of the teacher will vary significantly. Whether you choose a virtual school that is public, charter, or traditional, you can expect the teacher to be a very active partner in the education of your child. This is exactly the reason why many parents choose a public virtual option. They love the fact that they don't have to "go it alone" but will have the resources, including special education services, of a team of professionals—for free!

At the early elementary level, grades are not usually issued, but rather your child will advance based on mastery of the lesson objectives. In a public school, report cards are often required by law, but they serve a different purpose in a virtual school. The whole point of a report card is for the teacher to describe the child's academic progress to the parent. In a virtual school, you know your child's progress on a daily, if not hourly, basis. The report card will be used to show a future school (should you decide to stop virtual schooling) proof of your child's academic progress. Your teacher will be legally responsible for the education of your child and will check in with you periodically. On the other hand, if your child is struggling, you have a professional educator on the team who will meet with your child (either in person or electronically) to teach the concepts. Your teacher will also monitor attendance records and help design lessons appropriate to your educational plan.

If you elect to go independent, the responsibility of lesson planning, delivery, and assessment falls on you. Some private schools, such as St. Marks Academy (www.stmarksacademy.net), offer online courses with designed lessons, much like a public school would. By becoming a partner with you, programs like these free you up to do what you do best—teach and enjoy your child!

Co-ops take on the structure and mission of those who form them. Some parents prefer supplemental co-op classes that work well in group settings (like science labs, art, music, literature discussion, history discussion, and writing workshops). These classes can give parents additional help with subjects that can be challenging at home.

In the private model, parents can pay for trained teachers to be brought into the co-op to help with reading remediation, math tutoring, and other areas that are strengthened with expertise. In the public school model, the virtual school (charter, district, or state-based) will absorb the cost of providing the credentialed teachers to the learning center or co-op. Opportunities for learning, fun, and socialization are unlimited when, through virtual schooling, your family takes advantage of a world of options.

Many independent or private school parents form a "co-op" with different families to provide instruction, support, and accountability. The parents take turns planning the lessons and teaching the classes. A co-op usually requires that at least one other parent stay and help to facilitate the program. It is seen as an opportunity to get parents and children together, but does require more of a time commitment. This model is different than a "blended-model."

The main difference is that the community day program is part of a public school, so the parents can drop off their students like they would in a traditional school and the teachers design and deliver the lessons. The school organizes, sponsors, and takes responsibility for the program, including the cost of the teachers, facility, insurance, and instructional materials. Many parents love this aspect, feeling that it brings balance to their lives; they wouldn't enroll or feel as successful in a virtual school program without the support of a blended-model opportunity.

There are great common benefits in each program. They both provide opportunities for students to learn together, form relationships, have a social outlet, and learn from other adults, whether it be another parent or a certified teacher. "It is truly the best of both worlds" says Janet Aikele, former school superintendent, mother of seven, and virtual schooling advocate. A word of caution, however: Because co-ops are parent-organized they run the gamut in terms of quality. They can be truly enriching when planned and prepared for properly but require a lot of personal initiative. It does take time and effort in either model to drive your child to the site, and you have to balance the cost of the time and fuel with the benefits from the program.

Providing group learning and socialization opportunities is critical in the elementary years. Many different names exist for these type of programs, including parent co-ops, blended schools, and hybrid schools. Be a wise consumer and pick or help design a terrific one!

EARLY ELEMENTARY YEARS—THE BIG PICTURE

When you are starting to think about your child's elementary education, you need to break it down into the early and late years. There is such a wide disparity between the skills and needs of the early and late elementary-aged child that we divided the information by grades K–3, and 4–8. However, no matter how much your daily role changes as your child grows, you will continue to provide the direction and wisdom that will guide your child into adulthood. Understanding your son or daughter's cognitive, social, and academic needs during this time is critical for success.

The K–3 years will require the highest level of your involvement, time commitment, and pre-planning to ensure that your child's foundational skills are in place. There are many philosophies out there with opposing views about the start of "learning readiness" in children. Some researchers believe that the "brain is a sponge" before the age of eight, and therefore all of the foundational knowledge, especially for reading and math, needs to be in place by this time. Others feel strongly that the brain is still developing and that forcing a scripted curriculum on children is ill-informed and could lead to lifelong learning problems. So, who is right? And as a parent, whom should you believe?

Lisa and her husband, Scott, faced this dilemma with their children. Their oldest son, Brian, showed signs of "slow" development in language skills. His parents read to him nightly, played cassette tapes and ABC songs, but still he struggled with picking up words and constructing sentences. At age six, he was attending a private school with a small child-to-teacher ratio. The kids were placed in reading groups by color, and Brian told his mother that he was in blue, the "dumb" group. Concerned, Lisa devised a plan. She asked the school principal if Brian could attend school every other day, and she would homeschool him part of the week to help him become a more proficient reader. Lisa's vision for a "blended model" was born.

Unfortunately, it was 1989, and the homeschooling movement was in its infancy. Virtual schooling was nonexistent—the Internet was barely around. Yet Lisa was looking to "virtual education" to help. Because the school didn't feel comfortable allowing Brian to attend part time, she started her own "virtual school" at home, using computer games and learning programs during non-school hours. Yet at age seven, Brian was still not reading much beyond three-letter words. Then one day, Brian described to Lisa the main character in a new chapter book. Stunned, she asked him to read to her and he read fluently. He had mastered multisyllabic words, seemingly overnight! In school and at home, he had been acquiring the skills, yet not demonstrating them outwardly. This is the power of using a blend of computer-assisted instruction with hands-on projects, lots of great books, and a systematic approach to teaching the basic skills. This past June, Brian graduated from Harvard, demonstrating that he is now a proficient reader!

Virtual schooling allows you to take control of your child's future. Become passionate about researching and using different strategies for success. Stay focused. Be creative. Never give up and, especially in the early years, give your child the opportunity and exposure to great teaching with a rock-solid educational program. Your goal is to get your child to "grade level" and proficient in his building-block skills by third grade.

VIRTUAL SCHOOLING OPTIONS SUMMARY

At one end of the virtual schooling spectrum there are public virtual full-time schools, and on the other there is "going independent." Both of these options are 100-percent virtual. The blended version in the middle utilizes virtual schooling together with a face-to-face option, allowing for students to gather in the same physical location to enjoy learning together.

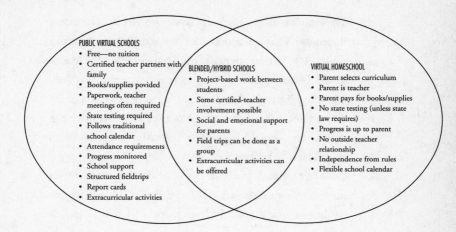

PUBLIC VIRTUAL SCHOOLS
- Free—no tuition
- Certified teacher partners with family
- Books/supplies povided
- Paperwork, teacher meetings often required
- State testing required
- Follows traditional school calendar
- Attendance requirements
- Progress monitored
- School support
- Structured fieldtrips
- Report cards
- Extracurricular activities

BLENDED/HYBRID SCHOOLS
- Project-based work between students
- Some certified-teacher involvement possible
- Social and emotional support for parents
- Field trips can be done as a group
- Extracurricular activities can be offered

VIRTUAL HOMESCHOOL
- Parent selects curriculum
- Parent is teacher
- Parent pays for books/supplies
- No state testing (unless state law requires)
- Progress is up to parent
- No outside teacher relationship
- Independence from rules
- Flexible school calendar

FOCUS ON KINDERGARTEN

To help you choose the right virtual program for your elementary school–aged child, we will explore readiness to begin kindergarten and show you a detailed plan per subject for this most important developmental stage. The rest of the elementary years will not addressed in as much detail, but you will get the idea and learn how to apply this system of selection to all of the grades.

Academic Development

For the beginning kindergartner language skills are being mastered at this level. Eye and hand coordination is developing and your child will learn how to complete fine detail work, such as using scissors to accurately cut out shapes and staying within the lines when coloring. Kindergarten lays the foundation for all future learning. If you'd like to measure your child's readiness, use the following assessment:

1. Does she know her ABCs? This will tell you if you need to work on some specific letters during her academic year.

2. Draw a circle, square, and triangle on a piece of paper. Ask her to cut around the outline of each shape.

Watch how she handles the scissors. Can she cut along the line? This measures her eye-hand coordination skills. Ask her to identify the shapes. Can she name them? If not, you will need to make sure she gets adequate exposure to them during her school year.

3. Show her a box of crayons and ask her to identify the colors. She should be able to identify all eight colors found in a basic box.

4. Give her a blank piece of paper and ask her to draw a person. How detailed does she draw? Does she include just the head, and stick figure for a body, or does she add facial features, hair, hands, and feet? The more developed her brain is, the greater amount of detail she will add to the body. You are looking for at least a head and body. Hands and feet are good, but if she includes eyes, eyelashes, eyebrows, ears, and hair, that is excellent.

5. Ask her to count—how high can she go? She should be able to count to at least ten. Most kindergartners can count to 20 and beyond.

When choosing an online curriculum for this grade level, look for flexibility in how the curriculum is delivered. You will want to select a program that encourages your child to be online less than 20 to 30 percent of the time. During the kindergarten year, your daughter should be able to finish her lessons in three hours or less, which means you should plan on her spending about 35 to 45 minutes a day at the computer. The rest of time should be spent doing fun projects and interactive hands-on activities.

Math
Learning math through hands-on tools such as building blocks, teddy bear counters, etc. is the way to go for kindergarten. Look for

a learning program that allows and encourages your child to have an adequate amount of "real-life, hands-on" learning time, including counting, grouping, playing with shapes, etc. One of the advantages of online lessons is how easily the computer keeps your child's attention. Matching games, mazes, and memory games are all great uses of the online technology.

Science

The world begins to open up to your child through exploratory, hands-on projects. Many parents ask, "How does science work in the virtual environment?" Lessons are presented in the online school, where your child can read about them (or at this level, be read to), see pictures, watch intriguing videos, and enjoy flash animation. Once she has finished the lesson, your daughter can do an "investigation" to discover in real life what she has just learned.

Hands-on lessons and investigations make science fun. Look for virtual lessons that incorporate "next steps" in the "real world." For instance, after learning about bugs in the virtual lesson, hand your child a magnifying glass and have him explore the world of bugs in your backyard. While the virtual lessons are designed to be proficient in teaching the skills, oftentimes adding a balance of hands-on activities will provide a more comprehensive experience.

The Internet is filled with curriculum suppliers, websites, and learning opportunities. The complete resource guide in Chapter 8 lists sites that you can explore to find the perfect learning tool for your child.

Social Studies

Where am I in this world? Where do I fit? What does a fireman do? Who is Abraham Lincoln and what is the White House? These are all questions your kindergartner has about the world. Do you think your child would rather read a book about the executive residence or take a video tour of the White House? The online school will introduce them to great American heroes and then suggest offline projects to reinforce not only the knowledge but developing skills.

Perhaps the online lesson shows a picture of a bald eagle and then suggests that you take your child on a nature hike to look for an eagle (or other birds as well), watch a video about the eagle, or have your child look for the eagle on everyday items such as our currency. Unit studies and learning around themes is the name of the game in kindergarten.

Language Arts

Reading, phonetic awareness (the ability to hear and identify sounds), concepts about print, decoding words, writing... these are all part of the skills that your child will learn in kindergarten. How is it accomplished in a virtual school?

The picture book comes to life as your child opens the online school and she meets Blue Robin for the first time. Walking through the pages of the book, she loves learning about the characters that Blue Robin befriends in the story. As she clicks through the screens of the online lesson, the sounds of the animals greet her. A PDF file attached to the lesson shows pictures of the characters in the book. A poem is also attached using the same animals. You print the poem and read it to your child as she colors the animals on the worksheet. Finally, she cuts out and glues the animals onto a sheet of paper and then writes the name of the animal under each, creating a masterpiece to be proudly displayed on the wall.

Music

As we mentioned earlier, 70 percent or more of your child's day will be spent in offline activities directed by online lessons. Music is one area that is mostly spent offline.

To teach the objectives of learning rhythm, beat, and notes, the online lesson will direct your child to listen to CDs and clap along, watch a video within the lesson, or play music games with friends and family.

Art

Art on the Internet? In kindergarten? If you're thinking that art is all about finger painting and making construction paper collages, think again.

Just because your child is taking an art class online, it doesn't mean that he doesn't get to finger paint, create collages, AND do so much more. He'll study Van Gogh, Monet, and Rembrandt. He'll view brilliant photos online and listen to stories of how the artists created their masterpieces.

Through the online lesson, your child will watch as the computer recreates how the artist painted or drew the picture, teaching her the foundational elements of art, including shapes. He'll learn about form, function, design, color, balance, line—all important artistic elements. Pictures of historical figures are presented to introduce portraits.

Your child will then reproduce the work of the masters using step-by-step directions and the skills he has just learned. It is a great moment to see the sparkle in your child's eyes as he compares the picture he just drew with the picture on the computer.

Social Development

Learning that the world does not revolve around the child is an important skill to gain in kindergarten. Make sure that your child gets enough opportunities to take part in group activities to learn how to share, solve problems with others, wait her turn, and learn how to play outdoor games appropriately. This requires you to take the initiative and seek out play groups, support groups with other parents, co-ops, or community day blended-model programs.

PUTTING ALL OF THE ELEMENTS TOGETHER

How can you incorporate all the learning objectives, cover the skills, and learn from the online school in a rich and engaging way? Let's consider a sample of skills to be covered (each skill below is typically a standard for kindergarten).

1. **Social Studies:** learning about maps and directions
2. **Science:** learning about mammals.
3. **Math:** identifying common objects in their environment and describing the geometric features.
4. **Language Arts:** reading and writing—knowing all the letters of the alphabet and using letters and phonetically spelled words to write about experiences, stories, people, objects, or events.
5. **Art:** Developing perceptual skills and visual arts vocabulary—recognizing simple patterns and identifying the elements of art (line, color, shape/form, texture, value, space) in the environment.

Your day may unfold something like this. At 8:00 A.M., your daughter is by your side, clicking to open the online lesson. The science lesson for the day introduces the different types of mammals found all around us. The math lesson introduces your child to different shapes—rectangles, triangles, and ovals.

You print the coloring sheet for your child to complete. The art lesson encourages your child to look around her environment to recognize different shapes and colors. The language arts lesson has your child reading a story about a picnic at a lake, and the social studies lesson is introducing your child to the concept of a map. It is 9:30, and you have already perused the lessons for the day.

Noticing it's a beautiful day, you encourage your child to draw a map showing your house and your local park. The online lesson introduced your daughter to directions, so you ask her in what direction she thinks the park would be. After packing a picnic lunch, you use the map to drive to the park for a fieldtrip.

You look for mammals that were discussed in the morning's lesson (deer, squirrels, cats, dogs, horses). You ask your daughter to identify the shapes found in nature—trees that look like triangles, the oval lake, and the rectangular picnic benches.

Next, your daughter draws the trees, lake, and picnic bench, identifies the proper colors and shapes, and writes the name below each picture. You remind her of the picnic that the character enjoyed in the story.

After lunch you set out on your science adventure to find as many mammals as possible and check them off the list. By 1:00, you are ready to go home and have not only enjoyed the direction, lessons, and ideas presented through the online school, but have enjoyed an engaging time of learning and relationship-building together.

Many activities can incorporate the lesson objectives for the day. The great thing about the online school—you don't have to worry about missing out on any of the foundational building blocks because the lesson designers (usually some of the most qualified teachers in the nation) have already done that for you.

FOCUS ON FIRST THROUGH THIRD GRADES

We have done an extensive job in presenting how the online program might work at the kindergarten level. You can use the model and concepts presented above to apply to any grade level. One of the most critical academic milestones occurs during this time. During the K–3 years, your child is learning to read. During the years of grade four to grade eight your child is reading to learn. Understanding the difference between these two is paramount to choosing the correct educational program for your child. As a child matures, the expectations of proficiency in the lessons mature as well. Your child's virtual lessons will emphasize the construction of strong language arts skills during this developmental stage. The lessons will continue to build a strong base of spelling, grammar, vocabulary, reading concepts, syntax, and language skills through the end of third grade. By the beginning of fourth grade, the lessons assume a proficiency level in the basic skills and begin to build comprehension and application skills. Less emphasis will be given to introducing the concepts, and more emphasis will be made on taking the foundation skills and using them to construct new meanings and develop advanced proficiency in subjects such as research, report writing, response to literature, and vocabulary. Do not be concerned when you notice the difference at the fourth-grade level. This is a normal development, but can be a little overwhelming unless you understand the academic development cycle. Your child will be expected to read for longer periods of time and you will see that reflected in the amount of material presented in the online school. As they move to the high school years, they will be taught to think more critically, develop persuasion skills, and apply all these skills to the workforce or to a higher education degree. But it all begins in the early elementary years.

Academic Needs

During the first grade, children are beginning to build on the skills learned in kindergarten. Kids enter first grade wondering how to write in a journal and leave being able to write several sentences in a logical order. Leveled readers present skills one at a time, beginning with three-letter words and rhyming words, and concluding with nonpredictable patterns and the ability to sound out new words.

Your child will graduate being able to read independently, write in his journals every day, complete complex grammar exercises, memorize poems, and recite from memory.

In math, your child will progress from understanding the concepts of ones and tens in the place-value system, adding and subtracting small numbers, and measuring simple objects to using patterns to solve difficult problems; tackling problems requiring addition, subtraction, multiplication, and division skills; and conducting simple probability experiments.

Cyber lessons can help you by providing an overall look at lesson objectives throughout the year. You can look in on the online school, click on the subject matter, click on "lessons," and view each topic to be covered. If you click on the topic, you can see the specific objectives within that lesson. This is a terrific help in understanding where your child is, and where your child needs to be.

Think back to a time when you threw a rock in a pond. The rock hit the water and created a circular ripple effect. Social studies is much the same way at this grade level. Your child's world will expand from learning about her place in the community to understanding the global universe. She will master map-making skills and understand how the various workers in the community provide the food on our table, keep schools open, offer medical services, keep us safe, and drive the big red fire engines down the street.

Science covers the area of physical, life, and earth sciences. Your child will learn to explore the universe around him through investigation and experimentation. Imagine your child starting a lesson about the ocean. It begins with digital photos so clear your child feels as if he is standing on the beach gazing out into the ocean. Next, he hops into his own imaginary submersible that takes him down to the ocean floor, stopping to study the light, temperature, and sea creatures along the way.

Once he reaches the ocean floor, he explores landforms and deep-sea creatures, and discovers how cartographers graph the depths of the ocean with sophisticated instruments. He learns vocabulary words during his underwater adventure, and then resurfaces to build a model out of clay and water.

The solar system, the water cycle, and weather are just a few more of the areas he will learn about.

Social Development

Your child is developing the capacity to build friendships at this age. She'll move from being egocentric to more socially oriented through exposure to groups, other children, and team-building opportunities. You need to make sure that your child gets enough opportunities to learn those skills through face-to-face gatherings such as community day, co-ops, sports teams, music lessons, choirs, Boys and Girls Clubs, church youth groups, and other great community clubs.

The great opportunity with virtual schooling at this age is that you can provide guided socialization opportunities and cross-generational influence. This is a terrific time for your son or daughter to learn manners, socially appropriate behavior (like being quiet during a performance), and how to carry on an interesting and detailed conversation with adults by involving family members and older adults to be a part of their social scene.

At this age your child will not yet have mastered the skills of working well in groups. Generally, kids will be either self-focused, quiet, distracted, or they will want to dominate a group setting. It's the extension of learning how to share—instead of just materials, games, and objects, they are learning how to share their time and responsibilities with others. They tend to be brutally honest when asked a question and still have a high regard for authority at this age.

Virtual School

You will see a dramatic change in the lessons presented during these years. At the first-grade level, you are expected to read the lessons to your child and they will do a lot of offline work. By third grade, your child is becoming much more independent and is now spending about two and a half hours on the computer.

Your role is to facilitate learning and make sure your child stays on track, plans her time wisely, and follows directions. You will still need to plan five to six hours a day to stay engaged with your child in her studies, but she will continue to develop more independence as she ages. If you choose a public school, they will be responsible for the overall academic progress of your child, issuing report cards; maintaining your child's cumulative file; providing services as needed, such as special ed and remediation; and supplying a credentialed teacher, administrative staff, and support programs such as community days.

As your child grows, so does the sophistication of the lessons. Never before has education been taken to this new frontier and the opportunities are endless.

FOCUS ON FOURTH THROUGH EIGHTH GRADES

Your child has now developed the learning skills necessary to begin applying them to a broader range of subjects, and is able to proceed with less direct help from you. Now that we have laid the foundation by explaining what to expect in the early elementary years, let's take the next step.

Academic Needs

We will be focusing on two academic areas: math and language arts. During this time, you will begin to see your child mature right before your eyes as they apply the higher-order thinking skills and foundational skills that were developed in the early elementary years.

In math, your child will grow in her skills from learning about fractions, decimals, and geometric figures to being fluent in angle measurement and the four basic arithmetic operations: addition, subtraction, division, and multiplication. She will master the compass, protractor, grids, tables, and graphs.

By the end of eighth grade, negative numbers, statistics, probability, mean, median, and mode make sense. Usually by the beginning of eighth grade, your child will be tackling algebra 1 linear equations and skills.

The biggest changes you will see during this time are the expectations of the curriculum and performance of your child. No longer is the learning program focused on teaching foundational skills. By fourth grade, the lessons assume that your child has those skills in place and will begin to direct her to use them in a more in-depth way.

Instead of learning to read, your child is now reading to learn. He will begin to develop analytical skills and learn how to write many different styles of essays from a response to a persuasive essay. Book reports are required. He will read several novels and begin to make his own decisions on what books to read.

Rote exercises such as spelling lists, vocabulary, and grammar drills begin to wind down, and by seventh grade your child will transition into exploring ways to apply knowledge. The goal at this stage is to move your child from a dependent learner to an independent one.

Social Development
The great pre-adolescent years are, perhaps, the most difficult time in any child's life. From friendships to bodies to hormones, everything changes during this time.

Relationships get more complicated as boys and girls find themselves attracted to each other and don't know quite how to handle those feelings. Keeping your child in a guided social environment through these years helps to relieve some of the social stress and allows her the freedom to focus on developing academic skills so that she can be more successful in high school and beyond.

Your child will begin to develop her online social skills as well. With e-mailing, blogging, IMing and text messaging, your teenager will quickly become fluent in the language of the day. It will be important to continue to give her face-to-face social opportunities and to monitor cyber usage. Many virtual schools and community co-ops offer student government, clubs, field trips, and community service opportunities for kids to be with each other, learning and serving.

Virtual School

At this stage, math lends itself well to be studied through an online course. Many courses will narrate the concepts for your child. Look for engaging, fun, and real-life applications within the lessons. For instance, your child can study the skyline of New York City and watch the lesson outline geometric shapes on the buildings, and then show how to measure the angles within those shapes—instilling the foundation for advanced geometry.

Some virtual schools offer fun online tutorial resources—such as Smarthinking.com or Study Island—to build and reinforce skills. If you choose to go independent, check out those resources; they do offer individual accounts to parents. Teachers, tutors, and online classes all are available to help your child master the math.

During the early primary school years, the lessons gave directions to you as the parent—"Read page 94–100 to your child and have her complete the project." During the later elementary years, the lessons will be written directly to your child, such as, "On the next few pages, read the biography of Martin Luther King, Jr. Be sure to write your response and reflections in your literary journal."

IT SOUNDS GREAT, BUT WHAT IF I HAVE TO WORK OUTSIDE THE HOME?

Don't immediately think that you can't enjoy the benefits of virtual schooling just because you are working outside of the home. Many people find creative solutions to accommodate both.

Some parents have jobs that allow flexible scheduling. Can you work two days a week on site and three at home? Can you bring your child to work? It is more difficult to try to balance an outside job with virtual schooling when your child is in K–3 because of the focused time required, but it can still be done.

Bring the grandparents into the fold. Both your child and his grandparents would love the opportunity to learn together. If you don't have family around, are there other families that you can collaborate with for child care and group instruction? Many parents enrolled in a virtual school with a community day use that one day a week as an opportunity to work at an outside job. Some families will hire a tutor/nanny and/or teacher to come to their home while they are at work to assist their children with their lessons. It's less expensive than private school tuition, especially if you are schooling multiple children at once.

Some parents put their careers on hold while enjoying what could be a far more productive career—that of being a home instructor to their children. Some moms start an Internet business, begin a home-based business, or work out an arrangement to telecommute.

Just like the Internet provides more opportunities for education, it also provides more opportunities for a global workplace. Facing a severe financial challenge, one mom, Linda, stood resolute in making the time to virtually school her children. In addition to loving her kids, she loved a great bargain, and Saturday mornings would find her roaming from one garage sale to the next in a hunt for treasures. She decided to start a business focused around garage sales.

She held quarterly garage sales, set up a table at the local flea market, shopped at garage sales, estate sales, and on Craigslist, and even started a consulting business to help others have successful garage sales. She published a newsletter and made herself available as needed. With that change, she was able to continue to virtually school her children.

Think out of the box—you don't have to work a nine-to-five job at an office to provide financially for your family. You know your family best. You know the feasibility of the employment flexibility and your situation. Our words of encouragement to you are: Don't be afraid to try something new and different to make virtual schooling work for your child.

WHAT MAKES A PERFECT VIRTUAL SCHOOLING PARENT?

If a child is raised in a house where parents are readers, chances are high that she will perform well on tests, according to a research project entitled the Early Childhood Longitudinal Study. The study followed 20,000 American children, collecting information on many aspects of their lives. The conclusion: Who we are as parents has a profound effect on the success of our children.

Today's generation of wired kids don't have parents who grew up tech savvy. So you are raising a revolutionary progeny—if your child is accessing technology to learn, they are virtual scholars. The question is, are you?

If we translate this finding about reading to accessing and optimizing technology and the Internet for our own lifelong learning, the continuing pursuit of career advancement, or following a passion we may have, what does it potentially uncover? An important component of preparing children for future success is that we as parents must model being a virtual schooler.

Learning is a lifelong process. Learning virtually is an interesting proposition, because as we stated earlier, this is the first time in history that our children are teaching us! We learn from each other and from the younger generation how to be tech savvy and cyber literate. Join your child in learning more about the technology that is most profoundly affecting their lives. Don't be afraid to play video games or to allow your child to teach you about the next and best computer program. Don't be afraid to venture into the social networking sites such as MySpace, Facebook, and MyYearbook.com. Learn about them—ask your child how they operate. Become interested in their world so that they can stay interested in yours.

There is no "perfect" virtual school parent—there is no "perfect" parent. However, there are parents who love their children deeply, invest in their future, and make daily decisions on how best to support their kids. Become one of those parents, do your research, make the most informed decisions—and you will be the "perfect virtual schooling parent."

CHAPTER 6

VIRTUAL SCHOOLING IN THE HIGH SCHOOL YEARS

Your child turned 14 and eagerly stepped onto the physical or cyber campus to begin his long-awaited high school years. Within a few short months you're saying, "what happened to my baby?" The adolescent years are challenging for everyone. As teens struggle with their ever-changing lives, parents struggle with understanding how to best support them.

But their emotions, mind, and body are not the only things changing. With the increasing dependency on the Internet to conduct business and facilitate social functions, their world is also changing on a daily basis. They need alternatives to the traditional approach of education to prepare them with twenty-first-century skills in order to be competitive in the global workforce.

It has become *critical* to utilize the time during your child's high school years to optimize his education.

As parents, we need to be sensitive to the differences in today's teenagers. With their technological realities and information delivered in hyper speed, many kids become overwhelmed, tuned out, and disengaged from the old style of education. They are trying to figure out who they are and how they fit into a rapidly changing world. At no other time is it more important to make choices about their education that will be relevant to them. Many parents turn to virtual alternatives to educate their children.

This book has introduced many approaches to virtual schooling: full-time virtual schools, both public and private; district-sponsored virtual school programs, supplemental virtual schooling to complement a traditional brick-and-mortar education; and blended or hybrid schools. Regardless of which approach you use, the added benefits of virtual schooling in the high-school years are immeasurable. They can aid your teen's entry into college, maximize interests and passions for early career exploration, and lay the foundation for lifelong self-directed learning. Additionally, by harnessing the power of virtual schooling you can save your family a significant amount of money by accessing available programs that reduce college costs, but not quality.

The flexibility and student-centric approach of virtual schooling also is efficient: It allows your teen to explore early graduation in order to attend college, and trains your teen to become incredibly proficient in a particular discipline, which could garner early college acceptance or increase the chances of landing a job in a stagnant employment market.

The approach to education in the high-school years is very different than that of the elementary years. Our teens are moving into adulthood fast. They have a stronger sense of self and of their interests and talents and are often technologically sophisticated.

While creating a personalized learning plan and accessing the best programs is equally important in the elementary years, our end goal of preparing our children for life as adults looms larger in the high school years. Therefore, our strategies for their education need to be even more flexible, include early career exploration, and require accessing a myriad of college planning and career planning—all in short timeline.

SELF-DIRECTING THEIR FUTURE

Most teenagers have access to just about anything by simply pointing and clicking. They are connected to all things digital and those digital connections give them power and control over whom they'll learn from, what they'll learn, and how they'll learn it. For the first time in history, our children are teaching us! They are driving the bus on technological change and letting us ride along when we can manage to hop on.

The proliferation of technology in our lives accelerates the independence of becoming a self-directed learner and broadens the number of ways that learning is accomplished. This means self-directed learning takes on an even more important role in the lives of today's teens. Not only must they be encouraged from an early age to take responsibility for their own lives and lifelong education, but we need to also help them learn how to disseminate, process, and tailor to their needs all the massive amounts of information to which they have access.

This might sound impossible, given that our teens often have a superior grasp of the digital world and new technologies compared to many of us. But as parents we must help them develop their expanded definition of a self-directed education to include critical-thinking skills. The complexity of new developments in education and understanding how to be a global citizen in our tumultuous world demands it.

NON-SELF-DIRECTED LEARNERS

The high-school years are critical in completing the academic construction project begun in kindergarten. As a parent, you have the responsibility to make sure that your child is receiving the best education possible in the most productive and successful placement. Every child's needs are different and some need to stay plugged into a traditional setting. For a variety of reasons, virtual education may not be the best choice for your child. If your child requires a lot of accountability and performs better with the daily structure of the classroom, it might be best to leave him at his brick-and-mortar high school. Some kids are just not good self-directed learners. They desire or require the personal touch of the classroom. Others even need the competition of their peers within the class to drive them to success. It's OK. Not everyone is cut out for virtual learning. Does your child love being in the marching band at school? If they are happy and progressing academically, perhaps it is best to not move them. However, if they want to stay plugged in at the school but would still like to be challenged academically, seek out supplemental virtual classes. At the end of the day, you will do your child a favor if he is not a virtual learner and you don't force him to become one. On the other hand, if you think he needs a change and can learn the skills, give it a shot!

SPECIAL-NEEDS CHILDREN AND THE HIGH SCHOOL YEARS

If you are blessed as a parent to have a special-needs child, you have probably already experienced the joy, frustration, and challenges of finding the right placement for him. As a parent of a special needs child, co-author Lisa tried private schools, public schools, learning centers, and homeschooling for her son, so she understands how discouraging it can be to try to find the right placement. Nothing can be more painful than watching your child try and try but not succeed at the same level as his classmates. As a parent, we are driven to advocate for our children and find the educational solution that will best serve their needs. Virtual education can be just the right solution if your child is easily distracted in the classroom, has ADD, or needs some extra assistance in acquiring skills, such as those a resource specialist would provide. However, please be cautious when hoping that a virtual education placement will solve all of your child's issues. If he doesn't perform well independently, this schooling choice may frustrate both you and your child. How do you know if your child is a strong candidate for virtual schooling?

Before virtual schooling was an option, parents had just two choices for serving students with learning, physical, or emotional disabilities. One was to mainstream them into a classroom where they would have received instruction aimed at the majority and then have some special services provided on the side, generally at the expense of removing them from their classroom for part of the day. The other was to place them into a classroom comprised entirely of other special-needs students, representing a wide range of needs, yet all being served together. Barbara Dreyer, president and CEO of a national virtual school provider, understood this dilemma and provided a solution by opening the virtual doors of the Connections Academy. Many students have experienced the success and power of personalized learning through schools like Connections. No longer must they leave the classroom to receive the one-on-one assistance they require. The virtual school is designed to support each student according to his or her specific situation.

Even with the personalized learning program virtual schools can provide, it is not the best placement for all students, cautions Mary Mertz, director of education for Insight Schools. Be honest with yourself and your child's needs when considering a move from his current school to a virtual program. Resist the temptation to jump on the virtual bandwagon thinking that it will be the perfect solution. In some cases it will, in others it won't. If you are considering a virtual school placement for your special-needs child, use the following questions as a guide to determine the best fit for your child's educational needs.

IS THIS A MATCH?

Personalized learning opportunities, individual pacing, and flexibility are great opportunities to support individual special needs. But how do parents determine a true goodness of fit when considering a virtual school placement? If a full-time placement is not the best fit, maybe a supplemental course would help your child feel successful, yet allow her to still benefit from the support of a traditional special ed program. Cyber courses can be especially helpful to students who need to work on their reading fluency skills. The following practical suggestions are provided as a first step in the decision-making process.

SCOPE OUT THE PROGRAM

Ask to preview a course or complete a course simulation. Have your child do the same. The time to discover whether this environment is the best is before enrollment, not halfway through the first semester. Interview the principal and ask to make an appointment to speak to a teacher. Ask if courses are differentiated—an education term to describe individualization. What support options are built into the courses? Is there an audio text that will read text aloud as your student reads along? Are there other supports for note taking and introducing vocabulary? Are there writing and editing tips as well as study skill suggestions built into the courses? Who are the special education staff? Ask the school for parent references you can contact to talk parent to parent.

UNDERSTAND THE REAL DEAL

Many students and their parents make false assumptions about on-line coursework. Most teenage technology experience includes gaming, downloading music, and social networking. While these are wonderful recreational pursuits, they are not alone representative of the virtual education experience. Yes, there will be wonderful synchronous sessions with social components. There will also be game-based lessons and practice. But there will also be reading. Students and families report back that they are shocked by the amount of reading involved in courses. The reality is that the reading is comparable to brick-and-mortar models.

IS YOUR CHILD A READER?

Think about your child's reading level. Most online courses are written at an eighth-grade reading level. The work will be difficult if your child is not at a solid sixth-grade level. The work will take much longer to complete. If your child is a strong visual learner who relies on visual cues from a teacher in order to understand the meaning behind the words, the virtual environment will be a challenging experience. If you feel that a virtual program is a good match for your child despite her current reading level, there are things that you can do to help improve reading readiness. Make sure your child is reading the newspaper every morning and discussing it with you. The paper is written at a sixth- to eight-grade level and can be a good predictor of successful online reading. Summer reading has never been more important if your child needs a reading power boost, and library cards are free.

BE TOTALLY HONEST WITH YOURSELF

Who is your teenage learner? Unless you yourself are planning to repeat high school, your learner must be able to work independently, or with minimal direction from you. This is an experience that allows a teenager to gain important independent skills that will follow her well beyond the high school experience. While adult coaching can be a strong support to your child, and your parent involvement will be appreciated, the diploma she earns must be her own. Let your child's online teacher teach and support the development of strong teacher/student communication. If your student is not an independent learner, what adult will be home and available to her to help establish the learning environment and monitor daily learning?

SCHEDULES ARE IMPORTANT

One of the appeals and strengths of virtual education is the flexibility it can provide students and their families. While flexibility is a wonderful thing, a routine and schedule are the building blocks of success. The routine and schedule may be morning, noon, or night—the only thing that matters is that there is one. The time frame doesn't matter as long as it is your child's optimal learning time and fits other family demands. Without a schedule, it is very easy for your student to fall behind.

COMMUNICATE CLEARLY, COMMUNICATE OFTEN

Your involvement and support in your student's learning is critical. Your active involvement provides structure and organization for your student. Begin with your child's IEP (Individualized Education Plan) and establish clear expectations. What is the specially designed instruction and how will progress be measured in this new environment? Establish a communication pathway and schedule for frequent contact.

NOT ALL MODIFICATIONS AND ACCOMMODATIONS ARE CREATED EQUAL

Understand that not every modification and accommodation currently on your child's IEP can be replicated in the virtual model. If your child requires intensive one-to-one support, or intensive modi-fications to the general education curriculum, the virtual environ-ment may not be the appropriate placement. Understand clearly the responsibility of your resident school district related to special edu-cation service delivery. This varies from state to state depending on the structure of the virtual program as a charter school, private school, or alternative program.

WHAT ARE THE CHOICES FOR MY SPECIAL-NEEDS CHILD?

If you choose to enroll in a public virtual school, they will provide the resources, help, and support you need. Private online high schools do not provide special education services, but often you can work with the teacher to adjust the lessons for your child. If you choose to "go independent" and virtually homeschool your child, you will need to make sure that you have all the support services necessary for your child to be successful. Many support groups and websites exist to en-courage, help, and train you to best meet the needs of your child

GETTING STARTED WITH SPECIAL-NEEDS STUDENTS

Check out Homeschool Central at homeschoolcentral.com. The website will provide you links for support groups, resources, practi-cal advice on scheduling and working through your day, home-school sites, blogs, and message boards. If you are interested in just finding out more information about special needs, visit the Special Needs Information Center at www.education.com or the National Institute for Learning Development at www.nild.net.

TWENTY-FIRST-CENTURY SKILLS

Have you needed information recently? How did you go about finding it? Did you pull out your trusty burgundy-leather-bound

Britannica, or did you do what our teens do when they want to re-search something—"Google" it?

If you Googled something, you probably received an astound-ing number of "hits" with a lot information on the topic. We quoted Wikipedia a couple of times in this book. (Additionally, we have created a Wikipedia entry about virtual schooling.) However, it was not long ago that Wikipedia was not considered a viable research tool, even though it came up high on Google results. Safeguards and auditing are in place now, and we have steadily increased our trust in the accuracy of the online encyclopedia. We now use Wikipedia as our aggregate source of information.

Educators recognize the need for our kids to be fluent in the digital language and many schools across the nation have launched initiatives to develop twenty-first-century skills. But what good are those skills if your teen doesn't know how to properly utilize and apply them? Enter critical thinking in the digital age.

Critical thinking skills give teens the ability to frame, analyze, and synthesize information in order to solve problems, answer ques-tions, and garner what they need for a project or interest. How do we help them do that? How do you ensure that the information you have acquired is accurate, unbiased, and applicable?

VERIFYING THE FACTUAL TRUTH OF WEB-BASED RESEARCH

Teaching those skills to your teen is essential in helping her build her digital proficiency, fluency, and application skills. Talk to your teen—show him examples of research, articles, blogs and posts you discover. Ask him to consider the source of the information and the likelihood of the intent of the author. Was the information founded in research or just someone's opinion? Does the author have a biased perspective? Teach your teen about domain names—information from .gov, .org, .edu sites would be more useful for their research purposes. Teach your teen to test retrieved information on trustworthy websites such as Snopes.com, which is dedicated to exposing urban legends and providing facts. Sound too good to be true? It probably is. Remember when e-mailing was new and you received a desperate plea to "please sign this petition" or "contact your Senator today—your freedom is in peril!"? As good citizens, many of us followed through only to find out that we had been duped. Lesson learned—and we need to teach the same lesson to our children.

KEEPING A DIGITAL-GENERATION TEEN INSPIRED

Across the nation, nearly five million high school students are not attending school. The Bill and Melinda Gates Foundation published a study in 2006 entitled "The Silent Epidemic," which states, "There is a high school dropout epidemic in America. Each year, almost one third of all public high school students—and nearly one half in some demographics—fail to graduate from public high school with their class. Many of these students abandon school with less than two years to complete their high school education." The reasons are diverse: health issues; teens who have become parents while in school; those who have to work because their family needs some extra income and can't manage a full-time school schedule; teens who need more challenging materials and, failing to receive them from traditional school, get bored and don't do the work they are assigned; and teens who just fail to make meaningful social or adult connections while at school. Virtual schooling can address many of these diverse reasons that cause teens to drop out or disengage from the learning process.

DROPPING IN VIRTUALLY

Keith Oelrich had to take action. He could no longer think America's dropout rate was someone else's problem. He knew many of the dropouts had a desire to finish school, but life had thrown them circumstances that forced them to give up on their dreams of college or a good job.

As an online pioneer and industry leader, Oelrich, founder and CEO of Insight Schools, had worked for over a decade in several online companies designing and delivering online courses in the developing virtual world, so he knew there was a solution to curb the number of dropouts. His commitment to providing equal access to all students regardless of their differences, life challenges, parental income, or dreams became a virtual school company—Insight Schools.

John was not your typical dropout. Maybe your family is facing some life challenges like John's family did. John's mother, a single parent, worked very hard, but she still struggled to make ends meet. John, age 16, was succeeding in high school and dreamed of going to college, but when his mother was diagnosed with cancer, he had no choice: He dropped out of school to earn money for the family. He thought about going to the local junior college or enrolling in night school, but that wouldn't work either: When he wasn't working, he felt he needed to be available to care for his mother.

One day he saw a commercial on television for Insight—a public online high school. John never knew before that he could attend a public high school, work with mentors, and take advanced placement courses online—and the virtual school would send him his own laptop to do so. Now John "goes to school" whenever he isn't working or caring for his mother. John is back on track to graduate and his dream of being able to go to college is now within sight.

CONNECTEDNESS

If properly organized, virtual schooling—both supplemental and full time—can provide many vehicles to allow teens to make personal connections with other students, with their teachers, and with school administration in ways that don't happen in many traditional schools. Brian Rose, SVP of Insight has seen this first hand. Working with urban youth in Portland, he saw the need for kids to connect to positive role models and the void left in many of their lives by the lack of them. He became passionate about harnessing the power of the Internet to provide critical connections for students to feel successful in school and in life. "If we change the future of just one student, we have succeeded," says Rose.

Co-author Elizabeth's husband, Michael, is a history and physiology teacher in one of the best traditional public high schools—Davis Senior High School located in Davis, CA. This is a university town where a higher-than-average number of high school students go on to a four-year college. The school was built for a student population of 1,000 students. Due to budget restrictions, Davis Senior High School now serves over 2,000 students. Not only does this overpopulation put a tremendous amount of pressure on the administrators and teachers, but it means that some kids will remain anonymous and make no meaningful connections to their teachers, administrators, counselors, coaches, or fellow students. If properly organized, attending a full-time virtual school or taking supplemental courses online can allow teens to make these vital personal connections.

"Online learning doesn't have to be an isolating experience," says Oelrich, "but rather a way of allowing students and families to participate in a thriving learning community." Full-time virtual schools have many of the same clubs as traditional schools, from math and language clubs to sports clubs, but they also offer a paradigm shift in that there is acceptance of things outside of what is considered "cool" or acceptable in traditional school. Because of the personalized learning and one-to-one interaction with teachers, mentors, and classmates, many students report that they feel that their online school knows them better than their traditional school did.

Stephen had a passion for politics. He became annoyed with apathy and the student government in his traditional high school. Once he joined a virtual charter high school, he found other students who were interested in leadership and had experienced similar frustration. They formed a student government club and began the political process.

The students launched a rigorous campaign, with candidates electronically campaigning, of course. Once elected, the new student government officers discovered they lived fairly close to each other. They decided to have their meetings in person once a month at a local bowling alley. After the meeting, they competed with each other in a friendly bowling match, building relationships while enjoying some physical exercise.

The club took on a life of its own. It grew to encompass talk about upcoming elections, political forums, the democratic process, and how running a student government in a virtual school is an excellent learning process that mirrors real life. The kids realized they are responsible for representing people that most of the time they never meet face to face. Therefore, they get a feel for the "real deal" and have to learn communication and representation skills to make sure that all voices are heard.

To gather the opinions of the student body, they accessed surveys in the WebQ (a web-based survey tool), posted communications in student forums, hosted threaded discussions, and used e-mail. Since they were the leaders of the school, they played an instrumental role in planning and executing the first graduation ceremony, complete with cap and gowns.

FRUSTRATION AND BOREDOM

If your child is struggling, frustrated in a class or school in general, throughout this book we've encouraged you to be an education consumer. It may take going to your teen's school administrators and advocating for an alternative, like Lisa did when her daughter Rebekah had trouble with algebra 2. As a parent-advocate, she researched several options and found that enrolling Rebekah in a private online high school was the right choice. Some counselors will be open, others won't. Don't give up. If the school administrators won't award the credit from an online course toward your teen's diploma, have her supplement the high school class, regardless. Exploring a subject online, where subject matter can be tailored to your teen's learning style and interests, can go a long way to improving his interest in the subject at school.

We've also created a comprehensive Virtual Schooling Resource Guide in Chapter 8 (a continually updated online virtual schooling guide is available at www.ivirtualschool.com). Hopefully it will empower you to work with your teen to find virtual schooling alternatives. Your family's lifestyle plays a significant part in determining if a full-time virtual school is a good fit for your teen, or if part-time virtual schooling might work better, so take the time to explore the options.

THE BEST-KEPT SECRET IN CUTTING COLLEGE TUITION

More than 1.2 million U.S. high schoolers will take "concurrent enrollment" courses this year at their own schools, online, and on local college campuses in different types of offerings. Concurrent enrollment means taking classes at two different educational institutions and having them both count on one transcript toward high school graduation. For example, taking a course at the local university and transferring the course credit back to the high school to meet graduation requirements.

New York State's community colleges are offering 60 classes this year to more than 100,000 high-school juniors and seniors carrying a minimum B-minus grade-point average. Students can take up to 11 credits per semester for $41 a credit—a third of the part-time student rate—with tuition breaks available based on financial need. In California, high school juniors and seniors can enroll for $1 a credit in junior college courses still open during late-registration periods. The state fills empty classroom seats in transferable general studies and major prerequisite courses that are often overcrowded at its public universities.

Madison Kanna's full-credit college course cost a whopping $5. However, the family savings on college tuition didn't start there. The Kanna family will have saved over $60,000 when their eldest, Randall, transfers to UC Berkeley or UCLA in 2010, after using concurrent enrollment programs both for real-time and on-line college classes, attending two years at her local junior college, and living at home.

Besides saving tens of thousands of dollars, concurrent enrollment programs help teens transition smoothly into college and can help your child follow a passion in extraordinary ways. Being allowed to pursue a passion early in a teen's education has the power to transform her future college experience and help determine her life's work. Not a bad return on a $5 investment.

PASSION

What can we do as parents to help our teen unveil his untapped potentials and passions? Use these clues to help your teen discover her true passions: What interests has your teen followed for some time? What subjects in school, activities, or hobbies does he get excited about? Author J. K. Rowling took an idea that popped into her head while riding a train—the story of a pubescent wizard—and created a world-renowned fairytale that in just ten years produced wealth surpassing that of the thousand-year-old British monarchy. What passions does your teen have that could be a well-chosen career or at least an engrossing college major?

MENTORING

Wikipedia's definition of "mentor" reads in part: "Today mentors provide their expertise to less experienced individuals in order to help them advance their careers, enhance their education, and build their networks." Wikipedia then lists a few well-known individuals who have benefited from mentoring: Richard Branson, Aristotle, Wolfgang Amadeus Mozart, Lance Armstrong, and David Beckham.

Only a relative few autobiographies penned by the most successful people in the world *don't* contain a story of how another's mentorship transformed their career or life's work. Additionally, in almost all career- and business-advancement books on the shelves today, you'll find the solid advice to find a mentor in the field you are interested in, whether it's someone in your industry or someone who has created a career in the area of your passion. Personal and professional coaching is increasingly popular for adults through mentoring programs. Yet, the power of mentoring isn't often accessed in the high school years.

Virtual schooling provides a tool with which to safely access mentors online or join a group with similar interests. Because attending a full-time virtual high school is so efficient, teens have more time to connect with adults in their own community to be mentored in a particular area for school work or to follow an interest.

A mentor can also be someone you know, or a work associate who helps your child prepare for success outside of any current curriculum. We can no longer assume that our teen's career success is a foregone conclusion with either a high school diploma or college degree, regardless of the pedigree.

Tapping into a full-time virtual school counselor, mentor, or tu-tors, both online and off, and thinking creatively to find potential mentors for our teens will provide lifetime skills not effectively taught in schools. It is all part of the power of virtual schooling for your high schooler.

FAST-TRACKING CAREER EXPLORATION

American workers lost more than $2 billion in retirement savings during the current financial downturn. As a result, many aging boomers will have to work and save longer, postponing their retire-ment plans and possibly blocking job openings for new and future college grads, says Mary Beth Franklin, senior editor of *Kiplinger's Personal Finance* magazine. "As workers scramble to rebuild their re-tirement nest eggs, they may have to shift their focus away from sav-ing for their children's college education. In this new economic environment, getting the most value out of higher education by uti-lizing virtual opportunities may trump the bragging rights of an Ivy League sweatshirt," says Franklin.

When we, as parents, include early career exploration in our teen's high school years, help uncover their passions, assist in finding mentors, investigate growth industries, encourage part-time work in prospective fields of study or careers, and instill in them twenty-first-century self-directed learning skills, we're doing our job—giv-ing them the support and tools to determine theirs.

SEVEN STEPS TO EARLY CAREER EXPLORATION

1. Educate your teenager to constantly ask himself throughout his junior and senior years as well as in college, "What do I really want to do?"

2. What career sounds exciting? Does she like the idea of landing a job that includes her interest in travel? Determining what they really want, or even determining what they don't want, can fast-track their career selection and success.

3. Help her figure out what she's passionate about. Tapping into a passion provides the power and conviction she'll need to break through barriers (fear, naysayers, and life situations) as she embarks on her career path.

4. His innate genius has given him talents that help him perform some things better (and with more ease) than anyone else. What are they? What possible vocation gives him the power to utilize those talents? Why have him spend years trying to figure this out, if he ever does?

5. Encourage him to research the fields, businesses, and industries he is interested in. Help him grow proficient in the "language" of the industry by reading trade publications and blogs related to his passions. Search out topics of interest at http://blogsearch.google.com and see who shares those interests. Determine the industry's growth potential in our turbulent job market and find out who the major players are and how they got where they are.

6. What work experience can she explore in high school or during college? How might she get paid to work part time in her dream field? Instead of taking the typical part-time job at Starbucks, have her consider an entry-level job that has more benefits than extra cash. Also, just because a position isn't advertised doesn't mean there isn't a job for her. Teach her to keep asking, "How can I?" This is an invaluable mindset for all areas of her life.

7. It's never too early to have him take an online class or acquire knowledge or key associations that can help steer the career when the time is right. Volunteering to help with community outreach programs and charity events provides real-world experience and builds more first-hand knowledge in his prospective field of study or industry. Teach him the power of expanding associations and connections. An introduction or meeting with a decision maker in a prospective field or area of study is often just what is needed to ignite an interest or lay the foundation for early career exploration. Plus, encouraging your teen to ask for help, seek out mentors, and gain more knowledge about a potential career now will help develop skills that will last throughout his entire career.

CHAPTER 7

YOUR VIRTUAL EDUCATION QUICK-ANSWER GUIDE

The previous chapters have presented many facts and ideas about how to make virtual schooling a reality. We hope they inspired you to take a serious look at virtual education as a high-quality option for your child. By learning how to leverage these resources, your child will be poised to enjoy a world-class education personalized to her unique talents and needs. The landscape of virtual schooling is changing overnight—so we have created this quick-answer guide so that you can keep the key points at your fingertips. Some of the questions are summarized here but covered in depth in Chapters 1 through 7. Others are simply added to provide a comprehensive foundation to the concepts and ideas presented within the book itself. To get at the heart of the questions most parents ask, we took to the virtual street and asked over 100 families to send us their tough questions. And here (drumroll, please)... are your top questions, asked and answered!

WHAT IS VIRTUAL SCHOOLING?

Virtual schooling is using the power of technology and the Internet to put your child, for the first time in history, at the center of the global education explosion. Virtual school does not mean schooling that only happens on a computer. It does not mean schooling exclusively with a full-time public school, or a part-time supplemental program, or an individualized learning charter school. Think of it this way: In the near future all students will learn through a *combination* of real-time and technology-based learning, and this will be the model of all education in the United States. We believe this new model of education, virtual schooling, is the nexus of engaged human involvement and the new delivery method of curriculum learning resources. **Accordingly, we define virtual schooling by the potential it holds: a personalized learning approach accomplished by leveraging the best of virtual and classroom-based schools or programs tailored to a child's needs and interests.** Defined like this, virtual schooling holds the potential to be the twenty-first-century educational approach that incorporates years of research with the power that new delivery method technology now provides.

WHAT ARE THE WAYS I CAN VIRTUALLY SCHOOL MY CHILD?

There are many different forms of virtual schooling, from supplemental (one class at a time) to full-time schools offering virtual curriculum. In Chapter 2, we discussed seven primary approaches to providing a virtual education program for your child:

- Approach 1—Personalized learning charter school

- Approach 2—Public virtual charter schools
- Approach 3—Local school or district program
- Approach 4—Going independent
- Approach 5—Supplemental programs
- Approach 6—Private online high schools
- Approach 7—The best of both worlds—hybrid or blended education

In virtual schooling, your child will have the opportunity to experience the best curriculum in the world. Lessons are designed to be engaging, current, interactive, and fun for kids. As your child grows, so does the sophistication of the lessons. Through the power of the Internet, your child can have the opportunity to have a pen-pal halfway across the world! If your child is learning about China, some courses include live sessions with kids from China to learn more about the culture, lifestyle, and language. Never before has education been taken to this new frontier and the opportunities are endless.

WHO TEACHES MY KIDS?

In a virtual setting, your child could have a team of experts available to assist him in the learning process. The degree of interaction with teaching adults really depends upon the method you choose.

PUBLIC FULL-TIME VIRTUAL (CHARTER, LOCAL SCHOOL— OR DISTRICT-BASED, PERSONALIZED LEARNING CENTER)

In a public virtual school (charter or school-based), the teachers are state-certified instructors who meet No Child Left Behind (NCLB) "highly qualified" status and are specially trained to meet the needs of your child in a virtual setting. If your child is at the elementary level, there needs to be a responsible adult available at all times to oversee the lessons. If you choose the public school route, you will be partnered with a credentialed teacher to make sure that your child understands the lesson, stays on track, and manages his time wisely. The beauty of the public school option is that the teacher assumes the primary duty of being responsible for the academic progress of your child, the curriculum is designed and delivered by educational experts in their field, and you get to do what you do best—enjoy the day-to-day learning experience with your child. The school also takes on the "legal" responsibility for educating your child, so although it is done in a home setting, you do not have to worry about keeping track of the records, audits, course credits, or accreditation.

PRIVATE VIRTUAL SCHOOL (FULL OR PART TIME)

Most private schools offer the same comprehensive course catalog as their public school counterparts. In most programs, you are paying for the courses and the teachers. Be careful, though, because some private schools are more like online correspondence schools than true virtual dynamic educational experiences. In some schools, the student is basically responsible for learning the material, much like in an independent study program. An instructor will grade examinations and essays, but other than that the student will have little contact with a teacher. In other private online schools, the teacher is available on a daily basis and assists the student with her lessons and delivers direct instruction. All private online schools are not created equal! Check out the quality of the staff, curriculum, and program. Generally, the cheaper the price, the less involvement you get.

GOING INDEPENDENT—VIRTUAL "HOMESCHOOLING"

If you choose a private full-time program, you can purchase the e-learning courses through a course catalog and assume full-time responsibility for teaching your child. If you choose virtual homeschool, you do not receive the support services of a public school (teachers, technology, special ed, etc.), but you do have more freedom to pick and choose the courses you would like and present them in a course of study that you design. Some virtual programs are sold independently to homeschoolers and include both online and offline textbooks, supplemental learning materials (like goggles and beakers for science experiments), and the online school, or Learning Management System (LMS).

SUPPLEMENTAL PROGRAMS

In most supplemental programs, you will enjoy the benefits of a state-certified instructor. In the public sector, statewide virtual schools and various state departments of education have begun to offer supplemental courses with teachers to complement a student's program. Designed with "exceptional" learners in mind, these programs aim to help students who are in need of credit recovery, live in rural areas and attend schools with a limited course catalog, need a flexible schedule, or desire to take a few classes online. In the private arena, supplemental courses are sold much like you would purchase a textbook. Sometimes you purchase just the online portion, other times you purchase an entire education experience, including a teacher.

WHAT IS THE DIFFERENCE BETWEEN "VIRTUAL EDUCATION" AND "VIRTUAL HOMESCHOOLING"?

Homeschooling is sometimes misperceived as moving the traditional schoolhouse home. The reality is that a lot of homeschooling happens outside the home. Similarly, virtual schooling is often taken to mean schooling that happens exclusively online. However, virtual schooling does NOT all happen on a computer.

Many educational methods used by homeschoolers are not found in a public school. In fact, many homeschoolers were early adaptors of virtual education who weaved it into a mix of methods and resources to suit individual children.

Virtual schooling is the new approach to education, encompassing all the ways that children can learn today. So, homeschoolers can be considered virtual schoolers as well, even if less inclined to choose a public school virtual program or curriculum. In other words, virtual education can be a part of homeschooling just as easily as it can be a part of a public school program. If you provide virtual courses to your children at home without being enrolled in any educational entity, including any public, private, charter, or supplemental program, you are virtual homeschoolers.

The two primary differences between independent and virtual public school students are financial costs and freedom in the educational plan. In the public virtual school, the curriculum is designed by curriculum experts and delivered according to state standards. In the independent model, parents have more freedom to choose—or create—any curriculum they feel is best for their children. The parent generally oversees the education and delivers daily instruction to the student. In virtual schools, the teacher oversees the education of the child, and at the high school level delivers direct instruction. Like everything else, there are benefits and responsibilities associated with both choices that must be considered carefully before making a final decision.

Public virtual schools are not "homeschools" in disguise. In the public school, the virtual version is tuition free and your child receives the full complement of support services, including partnering with state-certified teachers, receiving a technology package (including a computer and printer), accessing special education services that include testing, and participating in school-organized extracurricular events such as clubs, sports, assemblies, and student government. For many families, this is the first opportunity to have a computer in the home. However, it is not without the trade-off of less flexibility in curriculum choice and the pacing of the lessons.

Independent virtual homeschooling can incorporate e-learning courses, but should you decide to include them in your educational plan, you will pay for the courses. The flexibility that comes from not being tied to a specific program is appealing to some families. In exchange for the flexibility, you will be expected to spend more time designing, researching, and building the right program for your child, but the rewards can be inspirational.

WHAT IS THE DIFFERENCE BETWEEN A SUPPLEMENTAL AND A FULL-TIME PROGRAM?

In a full-time program, your child will be expected to take at least four core courses (science, social studies, English, and math) and can take up to three electives. Whether private or public, your child can expect to study between five and six hours a day to complete all the lessons. A supplemental program blends virtual lessons with some other form of schooling. Kids who are homeschooled or are attending a traditional school can enroll in a supplemental program for one or more courses. More students across the nation are enrolled in supplemental courses than full time, but that ratio is quickly changing as more parents discover the benefits and brilliance of virtual education. It is the best of all worlds—combining the power of the Internet with the passion of the kids to learn twenty-first-century style!

IS VIRTUAL EDUCATION HERE TO STAY, OR IS IT JUST A FAD?

Unlike other changes in education, online learning has grown rapidly in the last ten years. In the mid-nineties, the Internet was in its infancy and so was virtual education. Online learning has been growing at a pace of over 30 percent annually as people are realizing the power of this form of learning. Over 42 states offer some sort of e-learning (part and full time) and 26 states offer statewide virtual schools. In 2000 there were an estimated 40,000–50,000 students in virtual education and by the year 2007, that number had grown to over 1 million!

WHAT ARE THE COSTS AND WHO PAYS?

Public schools (such as Insight, Connections Academy, and K12, Inc.) are tuition free, so families can take advantage of the program without having to pay for the courses. These traditional and charter schools are funded through public funds based on attendance and enrollment.

If you prefer to go independent and virtual homeschool or enroll in a private school, the family incurs the cost of the program. The cost is driven by how you design your project. Parts of the program include the cost of the online course materials, subscription to the online school, student workbooks, teacher editions, supplemental kits (instructional supplies needed to complete the online lessons—such as science lab equipment, paint for art, etc), musical instruments, and a computer, printer, and Internet connection. Some courses, especially at the high school level, are sold as curriculum only, while others include instruction by a certified teacher.

There are other financial costs to consider as well. It is difficult to manage a full-time job and virtual school your children, especially at the elementary level. Many organizations offer training conferences and support groups to parents who want to school at home. When determining your budget, factor in the cost of travel, meals, and hotel and conference fees if you wish to attend. Tutors can be an additional expense if your child needs extra help, especially if you are choosing to go independent.

As many communities offer enrichment classes to students studying at home, check into what is offered in your area. Generally, you can expect to pay around $10 per class for art, sports, music, drama, and other enrichment activities.

If you do not own a computer and do not enroll in a school that offers them on loan, you will need to purchase a computer, printer, keyboard, mouse, and monitor. Many families opt for laptops instead of desktops as it opens up the possibility of staying mobile while schooling.

WHERE DO I LOOK IN MY COMMUNITY FOR ENRICHMENT CLASSES?

If you are enrolling in a public option, start by asking your teacher. Teachers usually have a full resource guide complete with programs, classes, and contact info within your area. If your teacher does not have a guide or you are choosing the private or independent options, call the following resources in your community:

- *Local Homeschool Support Group*
- *Chamber of commerce*—ask for a recreation guide for your city.
- *Department of parks and recreation*—usually they offer classes in three different sessions: fall, spring, and summer.
- *Conduct an Internet search for your specific need*—for instance, do you want to know where your child can take a karate class? Type in "karate class" and your city name into a search engine. Usually a listing of local classes will pop up.
- *Local public library*—The library will have a public posting area where classes and resources are listed. Talk to the

librarian. Introduce yourself to other parents in the library and ask if they know of anything.

- *Contact your local school district*—ask them if they have a resource guide. If not, ask for the name and phone number of the PTA president. They will provide you with contact information for one of the most well-connected parents in the community.
- *Contact your local churches*—many offer classes during the day for homeschooled children or they have a network of parents that you can contact.
- *The old fashioned way*—look in the phone book!
- *Even more old fashioned*—call your mom, talk to neighbors, drop by community centers, and ask if classes are being held or what resources exist in the neighborhood.

CAN I SAVE MONEY BY ENROLLING IN A VIRTUAL PROGRAM?

Absolutely! Think of the money (and time) you would save by not driving your child to and from school on a daily basis. In addition, if you choose the public school route, you will save on not purchasing curriculum or a computer.

WHAT IS THE ROLE OF THE PARENT?

In Chapter 5, Virtual Schooling and the Elementary Years, the role of the parent, child, and teacher are covered in depth. Here we will summarize those roles and add in the role of the school to give you an overall perspective.

As a parent, your primary role continues to be that of being a cheerleader, organizer, teacher, researcher, and your child's unwavering support group.

The first few common questions parents usually ask are "how much of a time commitment is required on the part of the parent?" or "who teaches my child?" or "can I do this if I am a single parent and am working full-time?"

See question below for a more detailed look at the time commitment associated with each choice.

WHAT IS THE ROLE OF THE STUDENT?

The role of your child is to love learning! No worries if your child is not proficient on the computer—with practice their skills will sharpen quickly. In fact, many parents report that their kids are more tech savvy than they are. The most successful students are self-motivated, enjoy learning on the computer, and can be disciplined enough to study and complete lessons on a daily basis.

WHAT IS THE ROLE OF THE SCHOOL?

The school is charged with taking responsibility of the "business" of running a school so that it relieves you of the burden of having to worry about all those details. The public school is responsible for offering a high-quality learning program, designing opportunities for students to interact, and providing teachers and support programs, including tech support, counselors for college and career guidance, and an administrative staff that is tasked with making sure that the school runs smoothly. The school must comply with the state mandates and statutes that allow them to operate legally. They will usually seek accreditation, select a governing board if it's a charter school, and engage parents to help plan the ongoing program.

Private schools have many of the same support services but are relieved from some of the reporting duties to the state as they do not collect state or federal monies.

WHAT IS THE ROLE OF THE TEACHER?

Depending upon which method you choose, the teacher will have different roles. In the public school, the teacher is given the legal responsibility of overseeing the education of your child and delivering direct instruction. Your teacher may visit you at your home or meet you at the school or any place that is mutually acceptable to both of you. Your teacher evaluates your child's work, issues grades and the report card, and makes sure your child is progressing through his or her studies. Teachers have to meet strict requirements, including being "highly-qualified" by NCLB (No Child Left Behind) standards; complete training to qualify them as online instructors; and have a passion for alternative forms of education. Teachers give assignments, teach in "real time" in the virtual classroom, and are your partner in your child's educational experience.

In the private setting or supplemental setting, the roles of teachers vary greatly depending upon the rigors and expectations of the program. Some programs don't have teachers at all and they just supply the curriculum. Others have teachers who are actively engaged in the child's learning, much like the public school, and still in other programs, teachers act much like "learning coaches." The best fit for your family depends on your values, academic needs, and the time you have available to devote to teaching your child. In going independent you assume the role of the teacher and your time commitment will depend on the age of your child.

HOW MUCH TIME COMMITMENT IS INVOLVED?

The time commitment of the parent will vary with the age of the child. At the kindergarten level, your child will require a lot of one-on-one attention and you can expect to spend four hours or so daily on school. By the high school years, your child will be much more independent and your role shifts; you'll spend most of your time assisting your child, supporting her and helping her to manage her time wisely. If you choose a program with teacher support, your child will be communicating directly with the instructor. As your child grows, the goal is to move her from being a dependent learner to an independent learner, with less time commitment on your part.

Look at table 7.1 on the following page to identify which option you might want to choose and the time commitment associated with each one. Each approach is presented and the time value in each column is *per week*. It takes into account the time that you will spend:

- Meeting with your child's teacher if you choose a public option
- Transporting your child to various activities
- Planning your time, schedule, and learning activities
- Completing educational activities including teaching, mentoring, tutoring, fieldtrips, clubs, assessments, etc.

HOW FLEXIBLE IS A VIRTUAL EDUCATION PROGRAM?

The beauty of virtual education is its flexibility. The lesson delivery schedule can be adapted to meet your child's individual needs. Your child can study algebra at 10 o'clock in the morning or 10 o'clock at night depending upon his or her schedule. The lessons are delivered whenever your child logs into the online school. Tutors and teachers are available online most any time. Imagine being able to design a learning experience for your child that includes an online reading about the foundation of our nation, a virtual tour of the White House, an online "talk" with Abraham Lincoln, movies about the Civil War, and a fieldtrip to Washington, D.C., to visit Ford's Theater and the White House in person. Your child can study and learn the Gettysburg Address from her online lesson, and then travel to

TABLE 7.1 PARENT TIME COMMITMENT PER OPTION

AGE GROUP	PERSONALIZED LEARNING CENTER	PUBLIC VIRTUAL CHARTER SCHOOL	LOCAL SCHOOL OR DISTRICT PROGRAM	GOING INDEPENDENT	SUPPLEMENTAL PROGRAMS	PRIVATE ONLINE SCHOOLS	BLENDED OR HYBRID EDUCATION (1-DAY-A-WEEK PROGRAM)
K–3	25 hrs	25 hrs	25 hrs	35 hrs	1.5 hrs/course	25 hrs	25 hrs
4–8	20 hrs	20 hrs	20 hrs	30 hrs	1.25 hrs/course	15 hrs	20 hrs
9–12	10 hrs	10 hrs	10 hrs	25 hrs	1 hr/course	10 hrs	10 hrs

the site where Lincoln delivered the address and recite it there while being videotaped. This is all possible with virtual education! Because the entire curriculum is available within the online school, you can manipulate the timeline to accommodate opportunities to combine virtual and real-life learning. Public schools adhere to a more rigorous schedule than private or independent schools, but still allow for flexibility in the program when approved by the teacher.

HOW DO I CHOOSE THE RIGHT CURRICULUM, PROGRAM, OR SCHOOL?

First, you must decide on the best fit for your family. Are you interested in full-time or part-time virtual schooling? Do you want a private, state-led, online charter, or district program? Are you looking for a school that offers a "blended" program, where your student can participate in on-site classes, clubs, activities, drama, sports, or music programs? For a complete explanation, see Chapter 2. Here are the main steps for determining the best program choice:

- Do your research—see Chapter 2
- Create a matrix—see Chapter 2
- Talk to other parents

Does the school offer an info session, a get-together, or an opportunity for you to meet and mingle with other parents at an open house? Ask the school, program, or curriculum company if they can recommend someone you can talk to. Understand, though, that they will only recommend parents who are highly satisfied and happy with the program; it can still be an enlightening conversation and help you to determine the fit for your child.

- Interview prospective programs—see Chapter 2
- Determine the structure of the program—see Chapter 2

- Match your needs with program offerings—see Chapter 2
- Is it all or nothing? The "blended program"

Blended models are emerging as the twenty-first-century option for providing the most comprehensive, engaging, and effective schools in the country." They may already exist in your community. Homeschoolers are taking advantage of onsite classes offered at junior colleges and community-based groups. District schools are offering virtual courses to their full-time students. Look for online charter schools that offer a "community day" or a "day on campus," which will provide your child with an opportunity to spend a day in a traditional classroom setting learning from a highly qualified teacher, interacting with their age-appropriate peers, and working in groups to learn group collaboration and problem-solving skills. Many programs will offer some relief for you as well! Parent support groups, training sessions, and "break time" are part of the program in many schools. Over and over again, parents say that the blended model is a life-saver for them, allowing them to network with other parents, share in responsibilities, and learn tools that will help them make more effective home educators and learning coaches. At the high school level, online charter schools are partnering with community agencies to provide vocational education. For instance, in Kansas, Insight School of Kansas is piloting the first online vocational class for high school students in collaboration with the National Center for Construction Education and Research (NCCER) and Crossland Construction of Columbus. Kansas is a progressive leader in the nation, allowing its students to dual enroll in virtual charter schools and attend their neighborhood school at the same time. For instance, if a student wants to enroll in a virtual school for their academics and still participate in the school marching band, they can do both.

WHAT ABOUT SOCIALIZATION AND SPORTS?

Our increasingly technology- and cyber-driven society is forcing us to redefine the process of socialization. In addition to expected face-to-face interaction, more Americans are using text messaging, e-mail, and social cyber sites, such as Facebook and MySpace, to "socialize." Socialization is generally not a concern for home-educated students. The community continues to offer opportunities for kids to get together in churches, scouting, drama classes, and play groups. People meet at the YMCA, Boys and Girls Clubs, and on recreational sports teams. With school violence on the rise, many parents may prefer non-traditional schooling models so as to screen out negative socialization.

Many online charter schools have taken socialization to the next level. In addition to offering face-to-face opportunities like fieldtrips, school events, and park/zoo days, they are providing chances for kids to interact online in the virtual classroom. "All-school assemblies" invite kids from all over the United States to participate and feature world-class guests such as Olympic athletes, Holocaust survivors, rock stars, senators, and filmmakers. Never before have such interesting guests been available on a monthly basis for kids to meet.

Sports opportunities are available to every student in the virtual school. Whether your child is taking part in a neighborhood game, playing on a sponsored recreational team, or training as a competitive athlete, every town offers some community programs for children. Several states have organized sports leagues for home-educated students. In South Carolina, for example, one group has organized a sports league of virtual and home-educated students. Fielding different sports teams, the kids practice and compete in a sanctioned league. In Georgia, a homeschool group in the Atlanta area has over

2,000 members and has organized their own league within the support group.

Some virtual high schools even offer a prom and graduation. There are so many socialization opportunities available that virtual students have to be careful to pick and choose so that they still have time to finish their lessons!

I'M CONCERNED ABOUT CYBER SAFETY— HOW DOES MY CHILD STAY SAFE?

The virtual schooling community takes teaching appropriate socialization skills seriously. It's a fact that kids are socializing online, and most virtual schools now require that students complete a course in cyber safety—whether it's for conducting research online or entering monitored online chat rooms.

However, you must be very proactive in monitoring your child's online use, no matter if it's for educational or social purposes. Here are a few recommendations to keep your child safe:

1. Install a network filtering software such as Net Nanny (www.netnanny.com). These software packages block websites, issue alerts for potential predators, supply social network user reports, and provide game controls.

2. Keep your computer in a public place. Watch them—look over their shoulder (even though they will hate it and you might be accused of "not trusting them"). Monitor their usage. If they are conducting their online usage appropriately they will have nothing to fear.

3. Check the "history" on your computer. Monitor the sites visited. If you are concerned, ask your child about it. Usually there is a reasonable explanation.

4. Keep communication open. As with most anything, open and honest communication is the key to success. If your child confides in you, try not to overreact but rather respond in a nonjudgmental way to keep the communication flowing.

5. Teach them to never give out any identifying information about themselves, such as a phone number or address.

6. Limit chat room participation to monitored rooms through the school.

7. Learn who your child's online friends are. Teach your child that not all "friends" are real. Don't ever allow them to meet an online friend in person unless you are with them.

8. Become one of your child's online friends. If they have an account in Facebook or MySpace, set up an account yourself and ask to be their friend. It will be a great insight into your child's world.

9. Spend time with them online doing fun things. Play games together and explore creative sites. Conduct a virtual makeover—try new hairstyles and makeup! Have fun! When you can experience fun and safe times together online, it will pave the way to monitor all online usage.

10. Don't ever be afraid to take control. You are the parent and the ultimate guardian of your child's social life.

WHAT ARE CLASS CHOICES?

A virtual program can generally offer a more comprehensive course catalog than a traditional school. The reason is that just like the students, the faculty is not bound to geographical restrictions. For instance, if a school wants to offer Mandarin as a foreign language option they must have enough students to enroll in the class and a teacher who is credentialed and lives within driving distance of the school. In a virtual program, the teacher needs to be certified in the courses that they teach, but since they are teaching virtually they can live anywhere. This is a tremendous asset! As an example, the French teacher at one online high school is also a French professor at a major university and is certified to teach high school. This is a high-caliber teacher that would not have been attracted to a traditional high school but loves the opportunity to teach a few classes in the virtual school.

At the elementary level, all four core areas (language arts, math, science, and social studies) are offered in alignment with state standards and cover the appropriate skills at each grade level. Electives generally include art, music, or a world language.

At the high school level, classes are offered in all four core areas (language arts, math, science, and social studies) as well as a host of electives including art, music, health, physical education, the arts, occupational education, world languages, and life and study skills. When you are doing your research and checking out different programs, ask to see the course catalog. While courses may change from program to program, some common examples of courses offered include:

Language arts = literature and composition, critical reading and effective writing, American literature, British literature, reading comprehension, writing and grammar essentials, journal writing, creative writing, mythology, journalism

Math = algebra, geometry, algebra 2, pre-calculus, trigonometry, and calculus

Social studies = world history, U.S. history, economics, U.S. government and politics, global studies, anthropology, geography, psychology, sociology (the study of human relationships)

Science = physical science, earth science, biology, chemistry, physics, integrated science, marine science, environmental science

Occupational/technical education = career planning, business communication, business and personal protocol, personal economics and finance, international business, communications/public speaking, computer fundamentals, digital photography and graphics, web design, Flash animation, digital video editing and production, C++ programming, game design, AP computer science

World languages = French, Spanish, Mandarin, Latin, German

Fine, visual, and performing arts = art history, digital photography and graphics, orientation to art, music appreciation, digital video editing and production, drama in literature, performance studio

WILL MY CHILD RECEIVE GRADES, AND WHO WILL GIVE THEM?

If your child is enrolled in a public virtual program, your child will receive grades and the teacher on record will be the one to issue them. The parent-teacher-student partnership is very strong in the virtual school and generally there are no surprises when it comes to grades and academic achievement as you can monitor your child's progress on a daily basis through the learning management system. If you choose the independent route you will generate the report card and issue the grades. If you choose a private program complete with instructors, they will issue the grades.

DOES A STUDENT EVER OPEN A "REAL" TEXTBOOK?

Yes! In many programs, textbooks are sent directly to the home to complement the online lessons. Several parents have remarked that it seems like Christmas when the boxes arrive and their child is greeted with high-quality books published by leading children's authors and reputable textbook companies. Some programs offer "e-books," which are electronic versions of the printed textbook. The beauty of this model is that the book is always with the student no matter where they go. No more excuses about losing the book—no more excuses about the "dog eating my homework." Ahh . . . the benefits of virtual learning!

HOW CAN I FIND AP COURSES NOT OFFERED IN MY TEEN'S HIGH SCHOOL?

Check with your local school to see if they have a partnership with a virtual program provider to offer supplemental courses not found in their course catalog. Many state departments of education will also offer AP courses through their statewide programs. Look up your state's department of education website and discover whether or not they offer a virtual program. Most private online high schools offer AP courses for sale.

WHAT ABOUT STANDARDIZED TESTS AND THE HIGH SCHOOL EXIT EXAM?

If your child is enrolled in a public virtual school he will have to take the same standardized tests, including the high school exit exam, as his traditionally schooled counterparts. If you go independent or choose a private school option, the choice will be yours. Many parents choose to have their children participate in the testing program as it gives a snapshot of their child's academic progress. Some test reports are detailed and can give you a strand-by-strand (for example, measurement would be a math strand within geometry) analysis of your child's performance. Just remember, though, that the test is a snapshot in time and may not be fully indicative of your child's abilities and academic achievement. It is one multimeasure that is used to gain the whole picture.

HOW DOES MY HIGH SCHOOLER DO PHYSICAL EDUCATION (PE)?

One of the most curious questions asked is how your child can do PE in a virtual setting. A child must have at least 20 minutes a day of structured physical activity and will record it on an activity log. Generally the PE or health teacher will design a conditioning program for them and then check in and monitor their progress. Some schools will send a heart monitor to your child to better track progress. Teens can participate in group or individual sports ranging from surfing to skiing to basketball. Check out your local gym. Do they offer free or reduced memberships to students enrolled full-time in school? Gyms have classes, aerobics, and strength-training equipment.

WHAT ABOUT COLLEGE?

Some parents might be afraid that by opting out of traditional schools they compromise their kids' future academics. They ask if their child can still get into a good college and/or get a diploma if they attend a virtual school.

Absolutely! Most virtual schools are accredited by national agencies. Common agencies include: WASC (Western Association for Schools and Colleges), NAAS (Northwest Association of Accredited Schools), and CITA (Commission on International Trans-Regional Accreditation). Coursework is accepted by major universities and colleges. Your child will get a diploma if she is enrolled in a full-time or part-time diploma-granting school. Many state-run virtual providers are supplemental and only provide course credit, not a full program granting a diploma.

ARE THERE COUNSELORS AVAILABLE FOR MY HIGH SCHOOL STUDENT TO HELP WITH SELECTING THE RIGHT CLASSES AND APPLYING TO COLLEGES?

In the public virtual options, a certified school counselor will be on staff to review your child's graduation check and help to ensure that she is enrolled in the proper classes. The counselors also are there to advise your child on future possibilities and college/career nights in the community, and help with the application process, if available.

WILL MY CHILD BE ABLE TO FIT BACK INTO A "REGULAR" SCHOOL AFTER BEING IN A VIRTUAL SCHOOL?

Curriculum designers have taken extra care to ensure that the skills and concepts taught at each grade level are consistent with those taught in the traditional school so that kids can matriculate back and forth, keeping up with their peers. In fact, since virtual education honors personal learning, many students use the opportunity to accelerate their learning and can skip a grade. If they are behind, it is the perfect opportunity to make up some credits to fit back into the regular academic program.

Teachers have noted that often students returning to a traditional program from a virtual one bring with them knowledge and a depth of understanding that contributes to the positive learning environment of the classroom. Your child might have to adjust to a more standardized time schedule, but generally the adjustment is an easy one.

WILL MY CHILD LEARN THE SAME THING FROM A VIRTUAL LESSON AS YOU WOULD FROM A CLASSROOM?

Your child will learn the same concepts, but in a different manner. For instance, if the science lesson called for your child to learn about the nucleus, cytoplasm, and cell membrane in a simple cell, a classroom teacher might begin the lesson (at the elementary level) by cracking an egg open on an overhead projector. The kids would all "eww and ahh," but then she would ask them to describe what they see. The yoke represents the nucleus, the egg white the cytoplasm, and the outer edge is the cell membrane. The students would then draw and label their diagram. The teacher might have a class set of microscopes for the students to then explore and discover different cell structures on their own.

In a virtual lesson, your child would see the cell come to life on the computer screen. Like watching a movie, she would see a cell being formed, and then she would be asked to draw and label the cell on a piece of paper. If you had a microscope at home, your daughter could continue the investigation on her own.

HOW OFTEN ARE THERE TECHNICAL PROBLEMS? WHERE CAN I GO FOR HELP?

Most full-time virtual programs have a highly skilled technology department. Trained technicians are on call to help you with any issues you might have. Generally, it's as easy as calling an 800-number for assistance.

CAN YOU DO THIS WITH MORE THAN ONE CHILD AT A TIME? IF YES, HOW?

It is tricky to virtually school more than one child at a time, but it can be done. We know of one mom who has 13 children (yes, 13) and she virtually schools 5 of them at once, ranging in grades from kindergarten to high school. How does she do it?

First, the family created a dedicated school room for their studies. She has a desk in the middle of the room. She was a homeschooler and then decided to go with the virtual school because she needed some of the workload taken off her plate so that she could focus on the daily lessons. The virtual school provided the perfect answer—lessons that were already created but flexible enough to be combined across grade levels. Their day is very structured and begins with chores, breakfast, and then saying the Pledge of Allegience. All of the lessons are reviewed the night before and the kids have a routine that they complete. Mom assists them at a designated time and then throughout the day as needed. She looks at areas in which she can combine different grade levels and enrolls her kids in those classes. Math and language arts are the most difficult to combine as they are individualized. Science, social studies, and electives are much easier to combine. The kids all complete hands-on projects together (even if it isn't in their specific lesson plan). Organization, structure, and wise time management is the key to success for this family. (And, oh, did we mention she had a baby and a toddler when she was virtually schooling her five school-age kids?)

If you have a toddler and are trying to virtually school an elementary student, take advantage of "nap time" and maximize it as a learning time for your older child. Also have a box of toys, crayons, coloring books, etc., that can only be used during "school time." This will help your toddler stay engaged.

WHAT IS A "MASTERY-BASED" PROGRAM?

Some virtual programs are "mastery based," which means that your child needs to understand the objectives of the lesson before moving on. In many classrooms, the lessons are progressed on a daily basis. This is terrific for some kids and not so terrific for others. Having your child study in a mastery-based program will ensure that their timeframe for advancement is individualized to them. As soon as they have mastered the concepts, they can move on! The program will not allow the student to progress if they do not achieve a minimum score.

IS VIRTUAL SCHOOLING LEGAL IN MY STATE?

Almost all 50 states offer some sort of virtual schooling options. Some states are more progressive and have fully embraced virtual learning and have all seven approaches available within the state boundaries. Others are slowly changing the educational landscape to include virtual schools. According to the iNACOL website, only six states do not have full-time, multi-district programs or "significant" state-led online programs. Those six states are Vermont, New Jersey, Maine, Rhode Island, New York, and Oklahoma. They do offer some services through consortiums, but not the comprehensive experience desired by most virtual schooling parents. All the other 44 states do offer some sort of virtual program. Check out the resource guide in Chapter 8 for more comprehensive information.

WHY DO STUDENTS LEAVE THE PROGRAM?

At the elementary level, the number-one reason why students leave the program is that the parent or teaching adult had to go back to work. Other reasons vary: the program was academically too rigorous, it was too hard with toddlers or multiple children, or there was a change in life circumstance—moving, job change, divorce, or death in the family.

At the high school level, some kids enroll in a virtual school thinking that it will be easy and then are surprised to learn that lessons have to be completed on a daily basis and teachers have due dates! Some leave because of life circumstances, others due to moving out of the area. And for some, it just isn't a good fit. It requires support, motivation, and self-discipline to have the best experience possible. Many students who leave are sad to do so and hope that they will have the opportunity in the future to, once again, be a virtual schooler.

IS THIS TOO ISOLATING FOR MY ONLY CHILD?

It can be. It depends upon your child, your family circumstances, and your initiative to provide community-based activities for your child. One family really struggled with this issue and the mom decided to have other kids over for group lessons. She was an art teacher, so it was natural to learn art together. She did feel a huge responsibility to be everything for her son—teacher, mother, and playmate. By fifth grade, they decided to make a change and she enrolled him in a site-based charter school. The first year was good, the second year, not so good. By seventh grade, he was (by choice) back learning in a home environment. With a constant flow of friends and fellow home-educated classmates, he is not feeling isolated—in fact just the opposite. He feels more enriched and free to pursue his academic and musical goals than he did when he was in the traditional classroom.

CAN I VIRTUALLY SCHOOL MY CHILD OVERSEAS?

Yes—anywhere there is an Internet connection, your child can attend school. There might be some restrictions on public school enrollment if you are out of the country, so check with your local school for their specific regulations. Generally, though, travel is allowed and encouraged while in a virtual program.

SO, WHY SHOULD I CONSIDER VIRTUAL SCHOOLING MY CHILD?

What a privilege it is to have the title "parent." We are entrusted with nurturing, educating, and forming a human life! There is no greater joy, challenge, and reward than to see your child develop from birth to adulthood. Virtual schooling provides the vehicle for your child to get a world-class education, learn twenty-first-century skills, involve you in the process, and create memories that will last for a lifetime. It is one of the most challenging jobs you will ever take on, but definitely the most rewarding.

CHAPTER 8

COMPREHENSIVE VIRTUAL SCHOOLING RESOURCE GUIDE

Within this chapter you will find over 200 sources for online education. At the time of publication the guide was up to date.

COST

F: Fee
N: None
O: Option

TYPE OF RESOURCE

1. Public virtual school
2. Private virtual school

3. Supplemental virtual program
4. Virtual classroom resource
5. E-learning course
6. Blended or hybrid program and school
7. iPod/iPod touch/PDA schooling such as iTunes U/ Also can be called Mobile Learning
8. Audio/visual schooling
9. Mobile schooling [we've named this emerging method of education for the first time in this book.] (Also check out www.mobileschooling.com.) #7 iPod/iPod touch/PDA category falls under mobile schooling.
10. Concurrent enrollment course and program

GRADES SERVED

K: Kindergarten
E: Elementary school
M: Middle school
H: High school
C: College

NAME OF COMPANY / SCHOOL AND PROGRAM	WEB ADDRESS	COST	STATEMENT	TYPE OF RESOURCE	GRADES SERVED
ipreppress	www.ipreppress.com	O	iPod download options include ebooks, language instruction, study guides to reinforce math and science concepts, famous speeches, and reference materials.	7, 9	M, H
Allied National High School	www.alliedhigh school.com	F	This accredited national online high school offers rigorous courses and diplomas for completion. Teacher interaction available but not required.	2	H
Apex Learning	www.apexlearning .com	F	Accredited site delivers online learning for credit recovery, remediation, and exam preparation.	3	H
Blueprint Education	www.blueprint education.org	F	Accredited courses for diploma, to make up classes, or to accelerate the educational process in order to graduate early.	2, 5	M, H

(continues)

NAME OF COMPANY/ SCHOOL AND PROGRAM	WEB ADDRESS	COST	STATEMENT	TYPE OF RESOURCE	GRADES SERVED
Center for Talent Development, Northwestern University	www.ctd.north western.edu/ learning	F	Housed at Northwestern University, this accredited program offers rigorous honors and AP courses for gifted students (based on SAT or ACT scores).	5, 10	E, M, H
Choice 2000 Online High School	www.choice2000.org	N	Available to five Southern California counties. Accredited, classes are in real time and mirror the traditional school day. Resources, lessons, tests, and teleconferencing available 24 hours a day.	1, 6	H
Christa McAuliffe Academy	www.cmacademy .org	F	Accredited classes are asynchronous and personalized for students' needs. School has flexible pacing depending on the degree of course focus, is mastery-based, and has assigned facilitators.	2	E, M, H
Clark County School District	www.csdde.net	N	For students in, and surrounding, Clark County, Nevada, this	1, 5	H

Virtual High School, Vigorous Online Learning Teaching Students (VOLTS)	accredited program offers interactive online coursework in a wide range of subjects.			H
Colorado Online Learning	www.col.k12.co.us	N	3, 10	
	Provides accredited supplemental learning for Colorado students through their school districts. Dual credit offered for select Colorado universities and colleges.			
Colorado Virtual Academy (COVA)	www.covcs. org	F	1	E, M, H
	A statewide, accredited Colorado virtual charter school using the curriculum from K12.com. Instruction is scheduled weekly and includes interactive online discussion with classmates and teachers, as well as use of alternative media.			
CompuHigh	www.compuhigh .com	F	2, 5	H
	Accredited online courses allow students to supplement learning or earn a high school diploma. Students are self-paced, teachers work one-on-one with students, with regular reports to parents.			

(continues)

NAME OF COMPANY / SCHOOL AND PROGRAM	WEB ADDRESS	COST	STATEMENT	TYPE OF RESOURCE	GRADES SERVED
Cyber Oregon Online CoolSchool	coolschool.k12.or .us	F	Online courses to complement Oregon public school courses. Courses are based on Oregon state standards, and include a wide variety, including AP.	3, 5	H
Delta Cyber School, State of Alaska	www.dcs.k12.ak.us	N	For students not attending an Alaska public school this public charter program gives students access to K–12 Alaska core curriculum. Web-conferencing and telephone access with teachers available.	1, 6	E, M, H
Denver Public Schools Online High School	denveronline .dpsk12.org	N	Accredited school instruction provided via Internet, broadcast television, and in-person tutorials. The school emphasizes teacher-student communication. Provides services for at-risk students.	1	H
HippoCampus	www.hippocampus .org	N	Offers multimedia lessons and course materials to help with	4, 8	M, H

Name	URL		Description		Level
			instruction, homework, and studies. Includes calculus, sciences, government, history, and more.		H
Education Program for Gifted Youth, Stanford University	epgy.stanford.edu/ohs	F	For gifted students only, this accredited program offers a rigorous curriculum for students seeking a diploma or additional advanced coursework supplemental to their public school offerings.	2, 5	H
iQ Academies	www.iqacademies.com	N	Available now in five states, this accredited online public school offers a robust offering of courses, including AP and world languages. Teacher interaction by phone, e-mail, and in person.	1, 5	M, H
Fairfax County Public Schools Online Campus, Fairfax, Virginia	www.fcps.edu/DIS/onlinecampus	N	For Fairfax County students only, this online program offers advanced courses in a number of subjects.	1, 5	H

(continues)

NAME OF COMPANY/ SCHOOL AND PROGRAM	WEB ADDRESS	COST	STATEMENT	TYPE OF RESOURCE	GRADES SERVED
Florida Virtual School	www.flvs.net	F	Offered to Florida students as well as non-Florida residents through Florida Virtual School Global Services, this accredited program offers a wide range of challenging courses, including AP and honors courses.	1, 5	M, H
Georgia Virtual School	www.gavirtual school.org	N	This accredited school offers basic and advanced coursework for Georgia students. Ideal for supplementing coursework for students attending smaller rural high schools. Students must log in four to five days per week.	1, 5	M, H
Greenways Academy	www.greenways academy.com	F	Accredited online coursework offered in a wide range of courses with one-on-one teacher support through e-mail and scheduled conference calls.	2, 5	E, M, H

Name	URL		Description		
Humanities and Sciences Academy	www.humscionline.org	F	This accredited program is rigorous and advanced in its offerings. Requires a minimum four hours per day and scheduled calls with teachers where students review studies using the Socratic method. Offered tuition free as an established charter school in Arizona, or for tuition for non-Arizona residents.	1, 2, 5	H
Illinois Virtual High School	www.ivhs.org	F	This accredited online program is for Illinois residents and is affiliated with the rigorous Illinois Mathematics and Science Academy. Wide range of coursework is offered to supplement student credits.	1, 5	M, H
Insight Schools	www.insightschools.net	N	This accredited online full-time, public, tuition-free school is available in ten states. Benefits are rigorous coursework and attentive, teacher-facilitated study.	1	H

(continues)

NAME OF COMPANY / SCHOOL AND PROGRAM	WEB ADDRESS	COST	STATEMENT	TYPE OF RESOURCE	GRADES SERVED
Internet Academy	www.iacademy.org	O	This accredited online public school program is free to students within Washington State and by per-class tuition for out-of-state and out-of-country students. Wide range of courses but no AP or honors.	1, 5	H
Maryland Virtual Learning Opportunities	mdk12online.org	F	This accredited online statewide program requires students to get guidance counselor approval prior to enrollment and a course fee is required. Full curriculum, including AP courses, is available.	5	H
Michigan Virtual High School	mivhs.org	F	This accredited online statewide program offers a traditional semester format as well as a self-paced format. Special research program allows advanced students to seek in-depth study on topic of choice. AP and robust course offerings are available.	1, 5	M, H

Name	Website		Description		
Minnesota Center of Online Learning (MCOOL)	www.mcool.org	O	This accredited online statewide program offers a wide range of courses, including AP and world languages. Available to nonresidents for a fee.	1, 5	M, H
Minnesota Online High School	www.mnohs.org	N	An accredited statewide online high school with a wide range of courses, including AP. Provides special education and hands-on teacher support.	1, 5	H
Mississippi Virtual Public School	www.mvs.mde.k12.ms.us	N	Statewide offering of a wide range of courses, including AP.	1, 5	H
Missouri Virtual School	mvs.missouristate.edu	N	Accredited program offers a wide range of courses to Missouri students, including AP. Synchronous and asynchronous courses available. School district pays fees.	5, 10	H

(continues)

NAME OF COMPANY/ SCHOOL AND PROGRAM	WEB ADDRESS	COST	STATEMENT	TYPE OF RESOURCE	GRADES SERVED
National University Virtual High School	www.nuvhs.org	F	Accredited program offers a wide range of courses, including AP programs, aligned with California state standards. Available nationwide. Teacher-led courses and access to extensive e-library.	2, 5	H
New Jersey Virtual High School	www.njvs.org	F	Accredited program requires students to get approval from their school district. Growing number of courses available, including AP.	5	H
North Dakota Center for Distance Education	www.ndcde.org	F	Accredited statewide program offers a wide range of courses from basic to AP and one-on-one teacher interaction.	1, 5	M, H
Northern Star Online	www.northstar online.org	N	Free to Minnesota students, this accredited program offers a wide range of courses, notably their Chinese Language Project in an interactive TV/online blended delivery system.	1, 5	K, E, M, H

Name	URL		Description		
Orange Lutheran High School Online	orangelhsonline.org	F	Accredited, rigorous program offers a wide range of courses, including AP. Full-time and supplemental program directed toward high-achieving students who have outside-class endeavors.	2, 5	H
Oregon Online	www.o2learning.org	F	Accredited coursework available to Oregon students and reimbursed depending on school district.	5	H
Portland State University Independent Study	www.istudy.pdx.edu	F	Accredited program available to residents and nonresidents. Wide range of courses available, including college level for dual credit.	1, 5, 10	H
Primavera Online High School	www.primaveratech.org	N	Accredited program for Arizona students with a wide range of courses through pre-calculus and honors English. Interactive and one-on-one regular communication from assigned teachers.	1, 5	H

(continues)

NAME OF COMPANY/ SCHOOL AND PROGRAM	WEB ADDRESS	COST	STATEMENT	TYPE OF RESOURCE	GRADES SERVED
Regina Coeli Online Academy	www.reginacoeli.org	F	Accredited online Catholic high school with a wide range of advanced courses available. Rigorous program taught with live conference software. Courses include twice weekly live online e-mail and audio meetings. Teachers work through scheduled meetings.	1, 5	H
Pinnacle Virtual High School	www.pinnacle education.com	F	Accredited program for Arizona students only for diploma and degree completion. Minimum 20 hours of work per week and no advanced courses available.	1, 5	H
PA Learners Online Regional Cyber Charter School	www.palearners online.com	N	Accredited courses available statewide in Pennsylvania with traditional online courses, AP, and real-time discussion board forums, live sessions, and frequent e-mail and phone calls between the student and the instructor. Seat	1, 5, 6	E, H

			time of five to six hours per day required by state.		H
Salem-Keizer Online	www.skonline.org	N	Accredited program for Salem-Keizer, Oregon, residents, and by tuition outside the district. Interactive program with teachers assigned for one-on-one learning. Wide range of courses available but no honors or AP courses appear to be available.	1, 5, 10	
Verticy Learning Academy	www.verticy learning.org	F	Accredited program designed for children with language-based learning differences, including dyslexia. Interactive, live tutoring, self-paced program, and Advisory Teacher Service. Utilizes the Calvert Program.	2, 5	4th–6th grade
South Dakota Virtual High School	sdvhs.k12.sd.us	N	Accredited program allows students to access a number of online state and regional programs and courses.	1, 5	H

(continues)

NAME OF COMPANY/ SCHOOL AND PROGRAM	WEB ADDRESS	COST	STATEMENT	TYPE OF RESOURCE	GRADES SERVED
Texas Virtual School	www.texasvirtual school.org	F	Accredited program offers a wide range of courses, including AP. Interactive and teachers and mentors are assigned to students.	1, 5	H
TRECA Digital Academy	www.tda.treca.org	N	Accredited program for Ohio students offering a wide range of interactive courses. iPods and other equipment provided free of charge for downloading lectures, speeches, and audiobooks.	1, 5, 7	E, M, H
University of California College Prep Online	www.uccp.org	F	Accredited courses available to students enrolled in California schools. Honors and AP courses available, and free supplemental, interactive lessons in science and math available.	1, 5	H
Lincoln Interactive	www.lincoln interactive.com	F	Accredited courses in a highly interactive environment with teacher access. Honors and AP courses available.	2, 5	E, M, H

Virtual High School Global Consortium	www.govhs.org	O	Accredited program available free in Massachusetts to students attending member schools and by tuition worldwide to individual students. Offers wide range of courses, including honors and AP. International baccalaureate program starting in 2009.	1, 5	M, H
Gwinnett County Online Campus	www.gwinnettk12online.net	F	Accredited program offering interactive experience, requires logging on four to five times per week. AP courses available.	5	H
Houston ISD Virtual School	vschool.houstonisd.org	F	Accredited interactive program available as supplemental coursework. Wide range of courses available, including AP and foreign languages.	5	H
Kentucky Virtual High School	www.kvhs.blackboard.org	N	Accredited program offering a wide range of programs including AP classes to Kentucky students.	1	M, H
Ohio Virtual Academy	www.ohva.org	F	Accredited public school program using K^{12} curriculum.	1	E, M, H

(continues)

NAME OF COMPANY / SCHOOL AND PROGRAM	WEB ADDRESS	COST	STATEMENT	TYPE OF RESOURCE	GRADES SERVED
University of Oklahoma, OU High School	ouilhs.ou.edu	F	Accredited program available, including honors, AP, and college level.	1, 5, 10	H, C
Kaplan College Preparatory School	www.kaplancollege preparatory.com	F	Accredited program available worldwide with advanced coursework, including honors and AP. Students benefit from one-on-one teacher instruction and demanding curriculum.	2, 5	M, H
UNL Independent Study High School	www.highschool .unl.edu	F	Accredited program available worldwide with advanced coursework, including honors and AP.	1, 5, 10	H
University of Texas, UT High School	www.utexas.edu/ cee/dec/	F	Accredited program offering a wide range of courses, including a program for English language learners. Multimedia and interactive courses available.	1, 5, 10	K-C
Virtual Virginia	www.virtualvirginia .org	F	Accredited program offers online AP, foreign language, and a few	1, 5	H

					non-AP courses. Courses provided in multimedia-rich environment with whiteboard instruction using video and audio clips. Free to Early College Scholars Program students.
Virtual Community School of Ohio	www.vcslearn.org	N	1, 5	E, M, H	Accredited program for Ohio students offers a wide range of courses and teacher communication via phone and e-mail and provides computer equipment.
Pennsylvania Cyber Charter School	www.wpccs.com	N	1, 5	E, M, H	Accredited program utilizing multiple resources and including synchronous and asynchronous learning. Advanced courses with extensive language choices, including Chinese and Arabic. For Pennsylvania residents only.

(continues)

NAME OF COMPANY/ SCHOOL AND PROGRAM	WEB ADDRESS	COST	STATEMENT	TYPE OF RESOURCE	GRADES SERVED
Utah Education Network, Virtual Field Trips	www.uen.org/tours/ fieldtrips2.shtml	N	This site provides images and information on a wide range of topics. Virtual fieldtrips include The Digestive Journey, the Violin Makers Shop Tour, and Japanese Culture and Stuff.	3	E, M
eduweb	www.eduweb.com	N	This site features digital games and interactive activities created for museums and other educational organizations worldwide in the areas of art, history, and science.	3	E, M
National Geographic Kids	Kids.national geographic.com	N	Kids learn geography, culture, and science through activities, videos, games, stories, and photographs.	3	E
National Geographic	www.national geographic.com	N	This site offers in-depth historical, cultural, and scientific education through photos, videos, text, audio, and satellite maps.	3	M+

Keystone National High School	www.keystonehighschool.com	F	Accredited, online courses allow high school and middle school students to supplement educational studies, earn a diploma, and/or prepare for college.	2	M, H
University of Illinois, U of I Online	www.online.uillinois.edu	F	Accredited, online courses allow for individual course study or completion of degree or certificate programs.	2	C
University of Phoenix, Online and Campus Programs	www.phoenix.edu	F	Accredited, online courses allow for individual course study or completion of degree or certificate programs.	2	C
Explorelearning, Gizmos	www.explorelearning.com	F	Narrated simulations of math and science concepts allow students to learn interactively and assess their understanding.	3	E

(continues)

NAME OF COMPANY / SCHOOL AND PROGRAM	WEB ADDRESS	COST	STATEMENT	TYPE OF RESOURCE	GRADES SERVED
DeVry University, Online College Programs	www.devryonline degrees.com	F	Accredited, online courses allow for individual course study or completion of degree or certificate programs.	2	C
North Carolina State University and University of Central Florida, Midlink Magazine	www.ncsu.edu/ midlink/	N	This site provides descriptions and contact information for students to participate in creative learning projects involving a variety of virtual media.	3	M, H
Mrs. Glosser's Math Goodies, Math Goodies	www.mathgoodies .com	N	Math support is offered in the form of interactive tutorials, games, puzzles, and practice sheets.	3	E, M, H
University of Missouri, Center for Distance and Independent Study	cdis.missouri.edu	F	Accredited, online courses from third grade and up allow for individual course study, high school diploma programs and programs for earning a BA of General Studies degree.	1	E, M, H, C

Name	Website		Description		
Your Digital Arts Cyber School, YDACS	www.ydacs.com	F	Online courses teach students to create digital artwork.	3	3rd grade–H
Sevenstar Academy, The Online Christian School	www.sevenstar academy.org	F	Online courses presented with a Biblical worldview allow students to supplement learning or earn a high school diploma.	2	M, H
Brigham Young University, Independent Study	ce.byu.edu/is/site	F	Online courses allow students to supplement learning or earn a high school diploma or a BA of General Studies.	2	H, C
Clear Ambition	www.clearambition .com	F	Online career and education guidance, including communication with a career consultant, provides support for professional self-discovery.	3	H+
Little Linguists Academy	www.littlelinguists academy.com	F	Children learn Chinese or Spanish from a teacher on video, mostly through songs and gesturing.	5	E

(continues)

NAME OF COMPANY/ SCHOOL AND PROGRAM	WEB ADDRESS	COST	STATEMENT	TYPE OF RESOURCE	GRADES SERVED
Professor Toto Language Education Series	www.professortoto .com	F	Interactive CDs and DVDs teach children French, Spanish, Chinese, or German.	8	Pre-K–6th grade
Personal Professors, Pre-College Math and Science Instruction	www.personal professors.com	F	Professors present lessons in higher math and biology and conduct live office hours weekly for discussion and follow-up.	4, 5	H
Smart Tutor	www.smarttutor .com	F	This site sells web-based software that provides interactive online instruction and assessment in math and reading.	3	E
ALEKS, Assessment and Learning in Knowledge Spaces	www.aleks.com	F	ALEKS software offers an assessment and learning system that ascertains a student's math knowledge base and adjusts instruction to suit. Higher education software is available in math, business, and science.	3	All

Holt McDougal	holt mcdougal.hmhco .com	F	Online books (e-editions) offer interactive technology in varied media. All academic subjects are covered, but hands-on algebra materials are most solidly endorsed.	3	M, H
eScience Labs	www.esciencelabs .com	F	Hands-on science lab kits with online content reinforce learning of key science concepts.	3	M, C
Spelling City	www.spellingcity .com	N	Teachers and parents can submit spelling lists for students to learn through games and fun practice methods.	3	All
DriversEd.com, Drivers' Education	www.driversed.com	F	Aspiring drivers can take driving courses for their state of residence and receive permit certification via mail.	5	H

(continues)

NAME OF COMPANY/ SCHOOL AND PROGRAM	WEB ADDRESS	COST	STATEMENT	TYPE OF RESOURCE	GRADES SERVED
ClickN KIDS, ClickN READ Phonics	www.clicknread.com	F	This online, interactive phonics program for both homes and schools provides instruction in letter sounds, word families, affixes, and more, along with progress reports.	3	K–3rd grade
Laurel Springs	www.laurelsprings.com	F	This distance-learning school with web-based communication and hard text offers a fully accredited education and supplemental courses.	2, 10	E, M, H
Alpha Omega Academy	www.aop.com	F	This distance-learning school offers computer-based, multimedia courses with a Christian focus. Diploma programs or individual courses are available.	2	E, M, H
homeschool-teachers.com	homeschool-teachers.com	F	Experienced educators teach AP courses live using audio/video,	10	H

Name	URL		Description		
YourOtherTeacher.com	www.yourotherteacher.com	F	text-messaging, whiteboards, and PowerPoint. This site offers online instructional videos, live tutoring with a whiteboard, and placement testing. Subjects are engineering, computer science, math, science, and elementary reading.	4, 5	All
The Learning Community International, eTeaching Assistance Program	www.etap.org	F	This accredited program offers courses with audio/visual instruction, interactive links, and hard text for supplemental study or earning a high school diploma.	2	K, M, H
Cramster, Cramster.com	www.cramster.com	O	This site offers "textbook-specific homework solutions" for math, science, and engineering textbooks used throughout the United States, as well as online study group support.	4	H, C
Oklahoma State University, eArchive Library	www.library.okstate.edu	N	This sophisticated database allows for in-depth research.	4	H, C

(continues)

NAME OF COMPANY / SCHOOL AND PROGRAM	WEB ADDRESS	COST	STATEMENT	TYPE OF RESOURCE	GRADES SERVED
Time4Learning,	www.time4learning .com	F	This site is an online home education program that teaches with interactive games.	3	Pre-K, E, M
Ablaze Academy	www.ablaze academy.com	F	Accredited, online courses allow students to supplement learning or earn a high school diploma. Live tutoring is available.	2	E, M, H
Calvert School, Home Schooling	www.calvertschool .org	F	This distance learning program uses textbooks and workbooks with online support.	5	K, E, M
Early Advantage, Muzzy BBC	www.early -advantage	F	This video program teaches language through animated stories and songs centered around the adventures of a cuddly space alien.	8	Pre-K, E, M
ED Anywhere	www.edanywhere .com	F	This accredited distance learning program allows students to	2	M, H

			supplement learning or earn a high school diploma. It also offers GED preparation and career counseling.		
Advantages Online Private School	www.Advantages School.com	F	This is an accredited, 100 percent online program offering courses that meet or exceed every state's standards. SAT and ACT preparation are available.	2, 10	2nd grade–H
Visual Thesaurus	www.visual thesaurus.com	F	Interactive dictionary and thesaurus that creates word maps to encourage creative thinking and word usage. Small monthly fee for online usage.	4	All
Connections Academy	www.connections academy.com	N	This accredited online education program is available in many states. Graduates are also provided with college- and career-planning support.	1	E, M, H

(continues)

NAME OF COMPANY/ SCHOOL AND PROGRAM	WEB ADDRESS	COST	STATEMENT	TYPE OF RESOURCE	GRADES SERVED
Global Student Network	www.globalstudent network.com	F	These non-accredited courses, available to schools and families, provide online instruction with ongoing teacher feedback and support via e-mail.	6	2nd grade–HS
Oak Meadow	www.oakmeadow .com	F	This distance learning school with hard text and online instruction and assessment offers a fully accredited education and supplemental courses.	2, 5	E, M, HS
Progress Academy	www.progress academy.com	F	This site offers online education in the form of e-books and interactive video learning. Students enroll annually by grade. Outdoor learning is also encouraged.	5	E, M, HS
K¹², Inc.	www.k12.com	O	This accredited program combines online instruction scheduled weekly, interactive online discussion with classmates and	1	E, M, HS

			teachers, as well as alternative media. Families can purchase K^{12} products or connect with a participating public school in their state.		
Texas Tech University, College of Outreach and Distance Education	www.depts.ttu.eud/ode	F	TTU is accredited and offers courses that are print-based, online, video, audio, and/or on CD-ROM. Students can earn diplomas or supplement study.	2, 10	All
Virtual High School of Excellence	www.virtualhse.com	F	This accredited school offers online education in the form of video, PowerPoint, Adobe Flash movies, and daily interaction with teachers via live chat rooms.	2	H
Let's Go Learn	www.letsgolearn.com	O	This online reading and math assessment program diagnoses a student's challenge areas, then recommends which of its products will solve the problem.	3	E, M, H

(continues)

NAME OF COMPANY/ SCHOOL AND PROGRAM	WEB ADDRESS	COST	STATEMENT	TYPE OF RESOURCE	GRADES SERVED
Bill Nye the Science Guy, Nye Labs	www.billnye.com	O	This site provides science instruction with directions on how to build science models and perform experiments at home. There is also a link to purchase Bill Nye science videos along with episode study guides.	3, 8	E, M
Rosetta Stone	www.rosettastone .com	F	This company offers instructional slideshows with audio in 31 different languages.	8	All
Indiana University, School of Continuing Studies	scs.indiana.edu	F	Students take online courses to earn a high school diploma or college degree or to supplement study.	2, 10	H, C
Instructional Video	www.insvideo.com	F	This site sells instructional videos and audio programs.	8	All
Talent Teacher, Art Lessons with Talent	www.talentteacher .com	N	This site teaches drawing, painting, sculpture, anime,	4	E, M, H

Teacher			landscape, computer graphics, and more.		
All Experts	www.allexperts.com	N	Inquirers e-mail questions and experts in appropriate fields reply. Links to topic-relevant websites are also provided.	4	M+
Oracle, ThinkQuest	www.thinkquest.org	N	Student groups with an adult coach work competitively to create websites on selected topics. Competition winners receive prizes such as trips, laptops, or digital cameras.	3	E, M, H, C+
Teach with Movies	www.teachwith movies.org	F	Learn through movie watching. Subscribe to this site to gain access to a library of movie lesson guides for history, English, literature, science, and drama instruction/ discussion.	3, 8	E, M, H

(continues)

NAME OF COMPANY / SCHOOL AND PROGRAM	WEB ADDRESS	COST	STATEMENT	TYPE OF RESOURCE	GRADES SERVED
Drexel University, The Internet Public Library	www.ipl.com	F	This site provides a searchable subject-categorized directory to websites and relevant links.	4	M+
Britannica Encyclopedia	www.britannica.com	F	This online encyclopedia informs through text, photography, video, and audio.	4	K, E, M, H, C
Sovereign Bank, Kids Bank	www.kidsbank.com	N	This website teaches kids about banking, saving money, accruing interest, checking, and other related information through animated characters, games, stories, and links to relevant sites.	3	E, M
Yahoo, Babel Fish	babelfish.yahoo.com	N	This website aids language learning by translating text in twelve different languages.	4	K, E, M, H, C
Crayon, Create Your Own Newspaper	crayon.net	N	Members of this website use the site tools to create a newspaper that can be modified and updated.	3	K, E, M, H, C

The Institute for Etymological Research and Education, Take Our Word for It	www.takeourword.com	O	This webzine features articles and answers to questions regarding word origins. Books on this topic are also sold.	3	M+
Merriam-Webster, Word Central	www.wordcentral.com	N	Reference this online dictionary, thesaurus, and rhyming dictionary for immediate results. Online word games also support language skill development.	4	K, E, M, H, C
Drexel University, Math Forum: Ask Dr. Math	mathforum.org/math_help_landing.html	N	Dr. Math answers specific math questions and offers an extensive listing of solutions to problems in every area of math.	4	E, M, H
WebMath	www.webmath.com	O	Enter any type of math problem into a pre-formatted problem page and get a prompt solution. This site also sells a homework help tool that is textbook specific.	4	E, M, H, C

(continues)

NAME OF COMPANY/ SCHOOL AND PROGRAM	WEB ADDRESS	COST	STATEMENT	TYPE OF RESOURCE	GRADES SERVED
Los Alamos National Laboratory, Mega Mathematics	www.c3.lanl.gov/ mega-math	N	Computative and analytical math problems are tackled in the form of multi-faceted projects with topic history, key vocabulary, hands-on activities and assessment. Topics include the math of knots, the paradoxes of infinity, and graph theory.	3	E, M, H
Science Academy Software, BasketMath Interactive	www.science academy.com	N	As students practice mathematical computation skills and problem solving, they earn basketball points.	3	E, M
Exploratorium, The Museum of Science, Art and Human Perception	www.exploratorium .edu	N	This museum site offers extensive online activities, exhibitions, webcasts, videos, and a digital library.	3	All
University of Saskatchewan, Exercises in Math	math.usask.ca/emr	N	This collection of math exercises are available for high school students who are preparing to	3	H

Readiness		enter the fields of higher math, science, engineering, or commerce.			
The Audrey Wood Clubhouse	www.audreywood .com	This site provides activities to enhance reading comprehension and enjoyment of such kids' books as The Big, Hungry Bear, Silly Sally, and Piggies.	N	3	E
Bartleby.com, Great Books Online	www.bartleby.com	This internet publisher provides e-books of countless works of fiction, nonfiction, and reference materials.	N	4, 9	M, H, C
Pink Monkey	www.pinkmonkey .com	This site offers study guides, book notes, plot summaries, and character analysis for 460+ major literary works.	N	4	MS-C
Web Museum, Paris	www.ibiblio.org/ wm	View hundreds of famous artworks with informative text on artists and historical periods. Also view the sites of Paris.	N	4	K, E, M, H, C
The Museum of Fine Arts, Houston	mfah.org	View famous artworks along with historical text and artistic analysis.	N	4	K, E, M, H, C

(continues)

NAME OF COMPANY/ SCHOOL AND PROGRAM	WEB ADDRESS	COST	STATEMENT	TYPE OF RESOURCE	GRADES SERVED
Kinder Art	www.kinderart.com	N	Intended to foster kids' love of and skill in art, this site offers art lesson plans, craft ideas, printables, and a teaching kit.	5	Pre-M
Google Earth	www.googleearth .com	O	View satellite imagery of every location on Earth, as well as maps and 3D buildings.	3	All
Castles on the Web	www.castlesonthe web.com	N	View castles, artwork within, surrounding countryside and native peoples from every corner of the globe, from Ethiopia, to Israel, to Estonia.	3	All
Simply Audiobooks	www.simplyaudio books.com	F	Rent books on CD and have them shipped to your home. Send them back when you're finished and order more.	9	All
Books on Tape	www.booksontape .com/cd.cfm	F	Buy books on CD or download audio off the website.	9	All

Children's Music Web	www.childrens music.org	N	This site provides resources for musical education to teachers, parents, and kids.	4	E
BBC, Learning Zone	www.bbc.co.uk/ learningzone	N	This is a viewing guide for educational programming on the BBC. Program topics include language instruction and geography.	8	M+
White House Kids	www.whitehouse .gov/kids	N	This site offers White House and governmental news, presidential biographies, videos, a freedom timeline and math challenges.	3	E, M, H
Fun Brain	www.funbrain.com	N	Students play web games to learn reading, math, and science.	3	E, M
Kids' Space	kids-space.org	N	Children can submit their own stories and artwork for display on this site.	3	E
Riff Interactive, Live Internet Guitar Lessons	www.riffinteractive .com	O	Learn guitar via the internet. Participate in weekly group lessons or pay for private lessons with a teacher of your choice.	5	M+

(continues)

NAME OF COMPANY / SCHOOL AND PROGRAM	WEB ADDRESS	COST	STATEMENT	TYPE OF RESOURCE	GRADES SERVED
Environmental Protection Agency, Environmental Kids Club	www.epa.gov/kids	N	Learn how to save the environment with interactive stories and games, project ideas, resources, and bountiful information.	3	E, M, H
It'sYourTurn.com	www.itsyourturn.com	N	Choose from over 60 games to play online at your own pace. Your human opponent will take her turn next time she logs in. No boards or downloads are necessary.	3	All
Strayer University, Online Learning	www.strayer.edu/learning	F	Online courses allow for individual course study or completion of degree programs.	2	C
Art Junction	www.artjunction.org	N	This site aspires to promote creative artistic expression and connection within the art community of students, teachers and artists. It offers activities, projects, artwork, links, and gallery information.	3	E, M

The Children's Museum of Indianapolis	www.childrens museum.org/ index2.htm	O	This site offers weekly classes for homeschoolers, games, and challenges relevant to the museum exhibits, and Science Port, an investigative project learning option.	3, 5	E, M
Cleveland Metroparks Zoo, Discover Plants and Animals	www.clemetzoo .com/discover.asp	N	Take a virtual tour of the zoo, learn animal facts, play games or contact experts at the zoo with specific questions.	3	E, M
Colonial Williamsburg, Electronic Field Trips	www.history.org/ trips	N	Younger kids will enjoy the games and illustrated stories about life in Colonial Williamsburg. The site also offers a listing of historical television broadcasts and podcasts, slideshows, timelines, and online exhibits.	3, 7, 8	E, M, H
TravLang, Foreign Languages for Travelers	www.travlang.com/ languages	N	Choose from over 50 different languages and learn basic vocabulary and pronunciation through audio.	3	M+

(continues)

NAME OF COMPANY/ SCHOOL AND PROGRAM	WEB ADDRESS	COST	STATEMENT	TYPE OF RESOURCE	GRADES SERVED
Amanda Bennett's Unit Studies	www.unitstudy.com	F	Unit study guides in the form of CD-ROMs offer cross-curricular instruction on a wide variety of topics.	5	E, M
PBS, Kids Play!	www.pbskidsplay .org	F	Kids play interactive learning games with their favorite PBS children's programming characters.	3	Pre-E
PBS	www.pbs.org	F	Buy PBS broadcasts of arts, drama, history, culture, and science programming.	8	All
Southeast Academy, Online	www.southeast.com	F	This online Christian school offers scheduled courses with required daily attendance and immediate teacher feedback. This is rigorous, not supplemental. Graduates receive a diploma.	2	3rd grade–H
Saxon Publishers	saxonpublishers .harcourtacheive .com/en–US/ saxonpublishers .htm	F	This site offers free online activities to reinforce skills taught in the Saxon Math and Phonics textbooks.	3	E, M, H

Name	URL		Description		
How to Learn Any Language	how-to-learn-any -language.com/e/ index.html	N	For the true polyglot, this site offers guidance, lingual and cultural information, links to instructional websites, and book reviews to enable self-learners to master any of 22 different languages.	3	M+
Free World U	www.freeworldu .org	N	This site uses superlearning (music) and electronic flashcards to reinforce learning in academic subjects.	3	All
Schoolhouse Rock	www.school-house -rock.com	N	This site provides the lyrics and the audio for all of the Schoolhouse Rock videos.	3, 8, 9	K, E, M
TM Books and Video	www.tmbooks -video.com	F	Buy the educational video series I Love Toy Trains and others from Lionel Trains and Boeing. Also available are the train exhibit video from Chicago's Museum of Science and Industry and the John Deere video series that teaches about tractors and agriculture.	8, 9	Pre-E

(continues)

NAME OF COMPANY / SCHOOL AND PROGRAM	WEB ADDRESS	COST	STATEMENT	TYPE OF RESOURCE	GRADES SERVED
Utah State University, National Library of Virtual Manipulatives	nlvm.usu.edu	F	This site offers a library of interactive, web-based virtual manipulatives, or concept tutorials, including learning evaluation.	4	E, M, H
Brain Pop	www.brainpop.com	F	Engaging animated movies and activity pages teach a wide range of content: academic subjects, health, arts, and technology.	8	K, E, M+
Tumble Books	www.tumblebooks .com	F	This site offers an online collection of animated talking picture books, read-along text with audio narration, and an online audio book library.	8	E, M, H
Starfall	www.starfall.com	N	Children build reading skills through phonics instruction, phonics-focused stories, games, and a collection of appealing reading materials.	3	Pre–2nd grade
Global Footprint Network	www.footprint network.org	N	Maps, graphs, and databases break down world resource	3	M, H, C+

Name	URL		Description		Grades
			consumption over decades. Students can take a quiz to determine their own ecological footprint in the world and consider solutions.		
Facing the Future	www.facingthe future.org	O	Aimed at teaching global sustainability, this site integrates environmental education with strategic objectives for civic action.	3	M, H, C+
Science Netlinks	www.science netlinks.com	N	In-depth science lesson plans integrated with internet resources provide hundreds of creative lesson guidelines.	3	E, M, H
The Genius Center	www.genieu.com	N	GenieU offers parent/teacher support and resources for tailoring education to nurture every child's unique learning style, intellectual strength, etc.	4	All

(continues)

NAME OF COMPANY / SCHOOL AND PROGRAM	WEB ADDRESS	COST	STATEMENT	TYPE OF RESOURCE	GRADES SERVED
Smithsonian Institution	smithsonian.com	N	Learn about science, culture, history, art, and everything imaginable by exploring the contents of any of the 19 museums of the Smithsonian. Kids learn through interactive online activities.	4	All
Mind Streams	www.mindstreams.org	N	Online education consultants help students determine course study directions and locate universities with concurrent (dual credit) or degree programs to fit their specific distance-learning needs.	10	H, C
NASA	www.nasa.gov	N	This provides education on anything related to space or U.S. Space Program. Options include photos, videos, informative text, podcasts, interactive activities, and a Kids' Club page.	3, 4	All

Massachusetts Institute of Technology	ocw.mit.edu/OcwWeb/web/home/home/index.htm	N	This site publishes the content for MIT courses. No credits or degrees are granted.	5	H, C
The Teaching Company	www.teach12.com	F	Buy instructional CDs and DVDs taught by professors from leading colleges and universities. Course options include liberal arts, business, math, and science.	3, 8	H, C
Penn Foster, Career School	www.pennfoster.edu	F	Students can earn high school diplomas or career diplomas/certificates through independent home learning, online or in combination with hard text.	2	H, C
techLEARNING	www.techlearning.com	N	This site provides resources and articles for educators who want to integrate technology with instruction.	4	C+
Kolbe	www.kolbe.com	F	Kolbe offers a variety of personal assessments to help one determine his/her natural inclinations and most effective methods of productivity.	4	H, C

(continues)

NAME OF COMPANY/ SCHOOL AND PROGRAM	WEB ADDRESS	COST	STATEMENT	TYPE OF RESOURCE	GRADES SERVED
ThomasArmstrong .com, Multiple Intelligences	www.thomas armstrong.com/ multiple _intelligences.htm	N	Learn to recognize your own or your students' individual intellectual strengths as they correspond to effective learning and teaching methods.	4	All
Pennsylvania Cyber Charter School	www.pacyber.org	N	This charter school offers asynchronous (self-paced) or synchronous (real-time) online courses. Students can supplement learning or earn a diploma.	1	E, M, H
Online Education Database, 100 Ways to Use Your iPod to Learn and Study Better	oebd.org/library/ beginning-online -learning/100–ways -to-use-your-ipod -to-learn-and-study -better	N	iPod learning opportunities include study guides, podcasts, tutorials, lectures downloaded on iTunes U, and much more.	7	M, H, C+
Online Education Database	oebd.org/	N	This database lists accredited online colleges and reviews online college programs.	4	C

Name	URL	Type	Description	Numbers	Level
RezEd, The Hub for Learning and Virtual Worlds	www.rezed.org/	F	This virtual education site offers internet-related podcasts, digital resources, and features blog posts and discussions.	3, 7, 9	MS+
Oklahoma State University, Project Advance	k12.okstate.edu	F	Through Project Advance at OSU, high school students can earn dual HS and college credit by taking courses online from their high schools.	1, 10	HS-C
iTunes U	www.itunes.com	O	iTunes U is a part of the iTunes Store and features free lectures, language lessons, audiobooks, and more.	7, 9	All
Hoosier Academy	www.k12.com/ha/	N	This public charter school is a blended model of brick-and-mortar and online learning.	1, 6	E, M, H

(continues)

NAME OF COMPANY/ SCHOOL AND PROGRAM	WEB ADDRESS	COST	STATEMENT	TYPE OF RESOURCE	GRADES SERVED
Olympus High School	www.olympushigh school.net/	Y	Olympus High School is a private online high school, built on flexibility and independence. All tutoring and school resources are online.	2	H
Horizon Charter School	www.hcs.k12.ca .us/	N	Horizon Charter School serves students in Placer, Nevada and El Dorado, Sacramento, Yuba, and Sutter counties in California. It is a personalized learning charter school with home-based/ independent study programs, a hybrid school, cooperatives, and Montessori options.	1, 6	E, M, H
St. Marks Academy	www.stmarks academy.net	Y	National online diploma granting Christian school serving students from grades 7–12 emphasizing leadership development	2, 4, 7	M, H

NOTES

CHAPTER 1

1. Eduventures. "What Can Virtual Learning Do for Your School?" September 2003, www.webct.com/service/ViewContent?contentID=17983410 (accessed February 2009).
2. Evergreen Consulting. "Keeping Pace with Online Learning: An Annual Review of State-Level Policy and Practice," September 2008, www.kpk12 .com (accessed February 21, 2009).
3. Ibid.
4. Center for Education Reform. www.edreform.com (accessed February 21, 2009). Note: There are 173 virtual charter schools with 92,235 students, up from 147 schools serving 65,354 students in 18 states in 2005–2006; 86 such schools with 31,000 students in 13 states in 2004–05; 60 schools in 13 states in 2002–03.
5. Tom Clark/WestEd. "Virtual Schools: Trends and Issues: A Study of Virtual Schools in the United States," October 2001, www.wested.org/online _pubs/virtualschools.pdf (accessed February 21, 2009).
6. Lee Rainie and Paul Hitlin. "The Internet at School," Pew Internet Study, August 2005, www.pewinternet.org/Reports/2005/The-Internet-at-School .aspx (accessed January 2009).

BIBLIOGRAPHY

American Optometric Association. www.aoa.org

Armstrong, Thomas. *In Their Own Way.* New York: Tarcher, 2000.

Bridgeland, John M., John J. DiIulio Jr.,Karen Burke Morison. *The Silent Epidemic: Perspectives of High School Dropouts* (A report by Civic Enterprises in association with Peter D. Hart Research Associates) Bill & Melinda Gates Foundation, March 2006

California Department of Education, "Charter Schools FAQ," (http://www.cde .ca.gov/sp/cs/re/qandasec1mar04.asp)

"Fast Facts About Online Learning," iNACOL (International Association for K–12 Online Learning, http://www.inacol.org/press/docs/nacol_fast_facts.pdf

Gardner, Howard. *Five Minds for the Future.* Watertown: Harvard Business School Press, 2007.

Garnder, Howard. *Multiple Intelligences.* New York: Basic Books, 2006.

Hackwood, Susan. 2008. Interview by authors. December 15.

Kanna. Elizabeth. *Homeschooling For Success.* New York: Warner Books, 2002. Levitt, Steven and Stephen Dubner. *Freakonomics.* New York: William Morrow, 2005 McKellar, Danica. *Kiss My Math.* New York: Hudson Street Press, 2008. McKellar, Danica. *Math Doesn't Suck.* New York: Hudson Street Press, 2007.

Science & Technology Index 2008. Milken Institute. http://www.milkeninstitute .org/presentations/slides/sos08_global_search.pdf

October 28.

Personalized Learning Foundation. (http://personalizedlearningfoundation.org/ _wsn/page4.html)

Pummer, Chris. "College-cost breaks." *Marketwatch (Wall Street Journal).* http:// www.marketwatch.com/news/story/picking-up-college-credits-maybe/ story.aspx?guid={03822CF8–571D–4946–8A97–540D65C4AF35}&dist= msr_1

Schank, Roger. *Coloring Outside the Lines.* New York: Harper, 2001.

U.S. Department of Education Institute of Education Science, "Dual Credit and Exam-Based Courses in U.S. Public High Schools: 2002–03." National Center for Education Statistics http://nces.ed.gov/surveys/frss/publications/2005009/index.asp?sectionid=2A

The Whitehouse Social Statistics Briefing Room (SSBR). "International Performance of U.S. 15-Year-Old Students in Science and Mathematics Literacy," National Center for Education Statistics, http://nces.ed.gov/ssbr/pages/pisa06.asp

Wikipedia contributors, "Mentor," *Wikipedia, The Free Encyclopedia,* http://en.wikipedia.org/wiki/Mentor

Yahoo! Media Relations, "For immediate release: Yahoo! Hotjobs big game plan helps job seekers discover their dream job," Yahoo! Hotjobs. http://docs.yahoo.com/docs/pr/release1206.html

INDEX